Written by Candlelight

Liesbeth Langford

*"I am so thankful to have discovered that you are still alive.
I was one of the children you rescued.
Just outside Jerusalem is the Anne Frank Park in which trees are planted
to commemorate those who helped Jewish children during the war years.
One of those trees is there because of what you did."*

**ERGO
PRESS**
Publishing for Northumberland

Written by Candlelight

Published by
ERGO PRESS

©Liesbeth Langford 2009

ISBN: 978-0-9557510-6-6

Cover graphics by Slim Palmer
www.slimpalmer.com

ERGO
PRESS
5, St Mary's Chare
Hexham
Northumberland
NE46 1NQ
ergo.press@yahoo.co.uk
www.ergopress.com
01434 689653

Written, published and printed in Northumberland

FOREWORD

As the Second British Army fought its way up the road from the Escaut Canal towards Arnhem, we were all conscious of the need for a quick advance, not only to join up with the troops fighting desperately around that town, but also to free the civilian population from their German oppressors.

Everyone in the Second Army had seen the privations which the French and Belgians had had to endure under the German occupation; I think we also understood that what the Dutch population had been, and were still being subjected to was if anything more desperate. The effectiveness of the Dutch Resistance was already being recognised.

In that last winter of the war, during curfew hours, Liesbeth Langford's English mother wrote down, by candlelight, what was happening around her while her husband was in hiding, working for the Resistance.

This book gives a graphic and very moving first hand account of the life of 'ordinary' people in Holland during the war. It illustrates the amazing courage, resilience and patriotism of the people, of all ages, during five years of occupation and shows their determination not to be worn down by their German occupiers.

The way in which Liesbeth Langford and her family coped with their hardships will earn the admiration and gratitude of every reader of this inspiring book and is a tribute to her parents' courage.

Major General Stuart Watson

ACKNOWLEDGEMENTS

I would like to thank Barbara Heywood who helped me with my English grammar in the early stages. Thanks also go to the many people who have heard my talks and encouraged me to write this book. Reproduced on page 141 is an orginal humorous postcard drawn by Arnout Gevers Leuven, to celebrate our liberation. Many thanks to Julia Grint, my wonderful editor. Working together with her was a joy and I felt just a little sad when it was all finished..."

My heartfelt thanks go to Britain and her Allies. I am proud to live in the country which gave us back our freedom, a country where respect for the individual is still the highest among many nations and a country which has given me a great deal of happiness.

Liesbeth Langford 2009

**For my husband Roger,
who was such a wonderful friend to my parents
and still is to me.**

November 1944
Heerenstraat,

My darling Jan Willem,

I can't do it any longer. The occupation has been going on for four years now, and it's really getting me down never being able to say even a single word in English because it's far too dangerous for us all. Thank God I learned Dutch as soon as we were married and I came to live in this country, and thank God I don't have an English accent when I speak Dutch.

So, tonight I have decided to write letters to you. Somehow I need to express my feelings in my mother language, and the only way I can do this is by writing them down. I love it. All of my pent-up emotions come rushing out and at the same time I can talk to you. Well, I can pretend I am talking to you, as I can't send you anything because you are in hiding; you had to change your identity and you have a false name and a secret address, and that will be the case for as long as you keep on working in the Resistance Movement.

Darling, I'll write letter after letter to you, telling you all the things that have happened and are happening in the frightening and dark world we are all living in, and each time I will carefully hide away what I have written. One day, my love, you'll be able to read it all.

Why do I write in English to my Dutch husband? Because that was the language in which we met. It was in the twenties, during the time when the dark clouds of the First World War had left our skies and when we knew nothing about the new storm that was to gather on a future horizon.

You were eighteen, you had just left school, and as your parents wanted you to improve your English, they sent you to Woodbrooke, the Quaker College near Birmingham.

Woodbrooke College

2

Your upbringing had been deeply Calvinistic, something you hated, and in Woodbrooke suddenly everything opened out for you. The Quakers showed you that it is perfectly possible to believe the way you wanted to believe and not the way a Dutch preacher thundered at you from a pulpit. You, who did not find it easy to make friends, made lots of them there, friends who were thinking the way you did. There was an atmosphere of deep religious faith, but there was also very much friendship, kindness and lots and lots of fun.

And there was me! This young girl from Surrey. You fell in love at once; I hesitated a bit, but not for very long, and that was the moment when my life changed totally. It's wonderful to talk to you in this way, remembering the past and writing down all the anxieties of the present. And we certainly had anxieties the other day, when Mary Jane and I tried to bring home some food parcels...

We were on our way back from a farm when suddenly I heard a noise behind me. I stopped, then slowly turned, clinging to the handlebars of my old bicycle with one hand and resting the other on Mary Jane's shoulder, trying to stop her from becoming too frightened. It was as I feared: German soldiers were marching towards the long bridge over the river IJssel. I realised straight away what this meant: the soldiers were going to patrol the bridge, and it could mean disaster. We had cycled 25 kilometres in a snowstorm to reach one of the outlying farms to find food. We had arrived, chilled to the bone, shivering in our woefully inadequate clothing. We are used to this; it is 1944, the hunger winter in Holland. This is the year in which desperate people are scraping dustbins in the hope of finding something to eat; this is the year when birdsong is heard no more in the West of the country, where the cities are: when you are starving, even small birds become food.

At the farm, in exchange for goods, we had received five small parcels to take home. We were lucky – this farmer had been generous. For one pound of butter he had wanted only my old watch. Compared to what some farmers ask for, this was incredible. He had given us the other four

3

small bits of food for some cheap jewellery.

Food transport is strictly forbidden. If you're discovered, you'll be sent to a concentration camp, if not worse. I knew that it would be impossible to cross the bridge with our parcels and there was absolutely no other way to get home. I had to make a decision at once; nobody just stood around with Germans approaching. "Go across the bridge, Mary Jane," I said. "When you get there, wait for me. Don't be afraid, the bridge is very long and the soldiers are only on this side; they won't even see you from here."

"But what are you going to do, Mummy?" Mary Jane asked. "Don't worry Darling, trust me and just go." For a moment I watched our fifteen year old on her poor old bicycle wobbling away from me. God, she was brave – but so many children learned to be just that, living under occupation.

I approached the first house I could see and knocked on the door. I had no idea who lived there. It could be a collaborator; there were plenty of those about… However, it was a kind, elderly lady who was happy to help. When she heard the story, she said: "The only way we can play this is by you looking different every time you take a parcel across to your daughter. I have an idea. I have lots of different coloured woollen hats and scarves. Take the first parcel and give it to your daughter, put on one of the outfits and come back to me, get the second parcel and change your hat and scarf again. There are crowds of people crossing the bridge all the time; those

4

stupid Germans will never notice."

And this is what I did. Each time I started off with a parcel, I could see Mary Jane as a tiny dot, patiently waiting at the other end of the bridge. Each time I heaved a sigh of relief when another outfit was undetected by the soldiers. Each time, going along on my stupid old bicycle with the tyres getting so very thin, I stared straight ahead, trying to look totally unconcerned. You really learn how to be an actress in times like these ... We made it. It took us hours, but we came home in triumph, with our shopping.

But, you know, this place is not really home; I long to be back in our own home in de Rozenlaan, the house that was taken from us just over a year ago by a German SS officer who thought it would be a nice place for himself. Ever since then, I and the two girls have been living with our wonderfully kind friends, who have given us two small rooms in their already overcrowded house: one living room and one bed room. The bedroom is just big enough for two, so I share that with Elsbeth, which means that Mary Jane spends her nights with neighbours across the road. Elsbeth sees it all as a great adventure. Well, she is only seven and it's good for her to 'tackle the war' in that way!

Before we were thrown out of our house last autumn we had already lived through a whirlwind of anxieties and events... 1943 certainly proved to be quite a year. I will never, ever, forget the dreadful day in May; it feels as if centuries have passed since then. You were still with us, holding down your job at the foundry in Vaassen, not far from here. You enjoyed the work, but there were problems: your uncle, who owned the business, had old-fashioned ideas about the way things should be managed, whereas you, being so much younger, wanted to introduce more up to date methods.

That brought difficulties enough, but there was a far greater and far more dangerous problem: there was a German engineer working at the foundry who was a keen supporter of Hitler, and he disliked you. This was partly because he regarded you as a threat to his own career, but even more because you were violently anti-German and made no secret of it.

5

Right from the beginning of the war, the Germans had forbidden the display of every kind of image of any member of the Dutch royal family. You loved your Queen, so nobody was going to prevent you from having a tiny photograph of Queen Wilhelmina on your desk at work. Well, somebody stopped you – it was the German colleague who reported you.

Queen Wilhelmina

And the following day, on a sunny May morning, you were arrested and taken by Dutch (!) police to be sent to a concentration camp in Vught, in the south of Holland. The police sent a messenger to our home to collect some underwear and a bible to take with you, and I went with him to the station and was able to say goodbye to you – how is any person able to do that at such a moment? I'll never forget going back home, meeting a loneliness and despair such that I hadn't imagined could ever exist.

A letter arrived from Vught!

Vught Concentration Camp

It was tiny, 20cm by 14cm, ruled and with your name, Jan Willem, under the printed word "prisoner", followed by the number 3728, Block 19. Quite a few other things were printed on the paper: in German it said that only the lines were to be written on, that each prisoner was allowed to write and allowed to receive no more than 2 letters or 2 postcards per month. Incoming letters were to be no longer than 15 lines on 4 sides and would have to be legible. If they were not, they would be destroyed. No money, photos or anything else were allowed to be enclosed. A huge censor stamp at the bottom of the letter made it very clear that each word was read by the camp's leaders.

In tiny letters was printed the following: "The day of discharge can not be determined yet. Visiting the Camp is forbidden. Requests for that are pointless." For me what was far more important was what the letter said; it was dated 13th May 1943.

> My darling Isobel,
> It is not so bad here. I have already made some friends.
> We are allowed parcels. Don't send butter or cheese, we get enough of that here, and don't send anything that needs to be cooked. I'd love some things to spread on bread and some rye bread and pancakes. Please could I have a nailbrush, and if possible, a little packet of toilet paper, a sturdy pocket knife, a block note, a small piece of soap and most of all, a letter from you. You know how deeply I love you but I'd better not write too much about that.
> We are also allowed money, but only by money orders. Could you send me 10 guilders to buy things with in the canteen? Be brave, that is what we do here as well, and tell the children to be extra good for you.
>
> 'Bye my darling,
> Jan Willem.

Mary Jane and I read and re-read the letter. You didn't sound too unhappy and conditions didn't seem to be too bad. Even so, the censor stamp at the bottom made it very clear that every single word was checked, so it was impossible to know what was really happening in that camp. When you said you had enough butter and cheese, we immediately knew that this would only be the tiniest amount, but then, we were all becoming used to smaller and smaller rations in our daily lives.

But you were allowed parcels! Mary Jane and Elsbeth at once started making huge lists and soon presents from neighbours, family and friends came streaming in. I oversaw all the wrapping; the sturdy knife was not going to be easy and everyone was rather surprised that this request would be allowed.

The most wonderful thing was that I would be able to include a letter. I would need to be careful with what I said in it, and Mary Jane would have to read it through and correct any spelling mistakes. One or two errors could give away the fact that the sender of the letter was not Dutch.

As I sat down after the girls had gone to bed, and began to write, it became a very special evening.

May 14th 1943
Heerenstraat

My one and only Darling,

Receiving your letter felt like a miracle! Both girls were dancing delightedly round the room, but I only sat still as I realised that I would open that tiny envelope and see your handwriting. How good it was to read that you are all right and making friends and that you aren't too uncomfortable.

It has been unbelievable here from the moment the news spread that you've been sent to Vught; the telephone has never stopped ringing and people keep on asking what help they can give us. We'll be able to send you some wonderful parcels, and Elsbeth says it will just be like a birthday for you, unwrapping all these goodies. She insists on giving up her sweet ration for you; she says, "I'll eat horrid food and then Daddy can have the nice bits".

Your mother is being wonderful. What a blessing it is that she lives in the same town as we do – she comes each day and helps with everything.

9

All of her friends in the home want to add things for you, so it's becoming quite a list! (She never likes it when it is mentioned that her home is one for elderly ladies!) Well, most of them are very plucky.

I miss you more than I can say and long, long for your next letter.

All my love, Isobel.

November 1944
Heerenstraat

My darling Jan Willem,

It is early morning, and I have spent much of the night remembering those weeks when you were in that awful camp. The early daylight makes it just possible for me to see enough to write; we have a few candles left, but we would never light one unless it were absolutely necessary, so I have waited patiently for the darkness to go and I've had ample time to think over what happened after those first few letters from you in Vught.

It was a beautiful spring day at the end of May '43 when the postman delivered a letter. We couldn't understand it at all: the address on the envelope was in your handwriting, but it was not the regulation tiny envelope used by the concentration camp. For a wild moment I thought you had been released or you had escaped, but no, it was a totally different story which began to unfold.

You explained that after you had been in the camp for a little while, it was realised that you spoke very good German (as if German could ever be 'good'!) and you were chosen for a job in the clothing department. The German who ran this department was a mild, gentle man who became so dependent on your organisational talents that he left it all more or less to you. Not only that, but through long conversations with him it became very clear that this softly-spoken man hated everything to do with the Nazis. He had grown up in a country he loved very much but had seen it change into something he could only be deeply sad and ashamed about.

He had seen the rallies; he had heard the screaming voice of his Führer; he had seen the cruelty meted out to Jews; he had seen some of his friends betraying their parents to the Nazi regime, because those parents were not as dedicated to Hitler's beliefs as they were expected to be. He had despised all of it, and now he was forced to give orders to people who despised him.

It must have been wonderful for him to find in you somebody who understood this, and perhaps because of that he did an unbelievable thing: he told you to write to me what you really wanted to say and he would smuggle that letter out and send it to me. And you, Darling, wrote it in English. Suddenly it was as if you were there, in the room, talking to me:

30ᵗʰ May 1943
Vught

My own darling,
(The contents of this letter must not go beyond you.)
There's a chance of getting this out and I just want to tell you that all is well. Thank you for the lovely parcels; I've had 6 up to now.

Yesterday's parcel had your message "Here all is well" on the inside of the lid and a guilder in the cake. What a lovely way of hiding a guilder! It reminded me of spending Christmas with your parents and all the English traditions I had to learn.

Don't send me any more articles of clothing or hankies or anything permanent – I can manage with what I've got and too many possessions is just a nuisance here.

A bit of soap and a kitchen spoon is all I need. And

many smaller parcels of food (like you are sending now, twice a week), is better than a few big ones.

I have made many friends here – there are some ripping ones, although the company is very mixed.

I've got office work in the clothing department, so that I don't have to do the often hard, physical labour. That is because I can use a type-writer and know some German. I work under a non-commissioned SS man, who is friendly, elderly, pleasant and polite. I know already much more about his work than he does ...

The days are long – Reveille at 5. Parade at 5.30. Work 6-12. Parade until 12.15. Dinner. Work 1-6. Parade until 6.30. Supper. After supper free. To bed at 9.

That gives very little time for spiritual luxuries like a worthwhile talk about things that matter – or physical things, like a shave…

I was heard by the Sicherheits Dienst (Security Office) the other day. (Keep this a dead secret from everybody – this is serious!) I am accused of Anti-German Propaganda, though they only mentioned the Queen's photograph at the foundry, the day I was arrested.

They beat me until I "confessed". Of course, they knew from the start that I hate the German propaganda as much as they love it. But they had to prove their point.

I am rather afraid that this will mean a fairly lengthy stay here. I never think of chances of being let out. I just accept life as it comes. Apart from that I am very much alive (and near to God) – I miss you very much, but I simply force myself not to think about my life "outside" – I'm terrified of homesickness, that is a fatal disease here.

Kiss Moeder and the children from me. Must stop in a hurry – all my love my dearest darling,   Jan Willem.

PS Things like anchovy paste and jam are very welcome and chocolate if you can spare some.

PPS There is just time to add a line. Are you really all right? Is Mary Jane doing her best at school and piano? How is her tennis getting on? Little Elsbeth good? No nail biting or thumb sucking? Send me a small note like you did with the guilder at the bottom of a parcel or something. I must not let myself love you here, but I do darling, like never before.

J. W.

Enclosed with the letter was a tiny note in an unknown German hand:

"I send you your husband's letter because I like and admire him. Through what he told me about you, I also admire you. I am deeply sorry, but I will not be able to send any more, it is too dangerous and not only for me. May I wish you God's blessing."

I will keep that note, and hide it away with all my letters.

December 1944
Heerenstraat

Darling Jan Willem,

This morning I was lying in bed, missing you the way I do every time I wake up, so I have decided that I will try and write down for you how each day begins:

Picture the scene, My Love: it is still pitch dark, but it must be nearly day-time, for Anneke, the baby of the family with whom we are living, is making her usual early morning noises. She is the youngest of five and she is a very reliable substitute for the watch I exchanged for that pound of butter a few weeks ago. It is about 7am, but it won't be light for at least another hour, so it is no use getting up yet. Our few remaining candles are very precious; we would never consider lighting one in the morning. We have had no gas or electricity for several months now and we are quite used to going to bed at 7.30 in the evening and getting up at 8.30 the next morning, spending several hours in bed just thinking…

At last a faint glimmer of light appears, and soon I get up and dress. The warmth of yesterday's fire has not quite left the room, but all the same I put on my old coat, because it is freezing hard outside and we can't afford to light the fire until noon: we have absolutely no coal left; the only fuel is damp wood. Most people have to go into the woods and cut down trees, but I am fortunate; a friend has provided us with some large logs. Mary Jane chops them into small ones – this is one of her regular jobs and it keeps her warm for at least part of the day.

Breakfast consists of lukewarm porridge – no sugar of course – and two very thin slices of a brownish, grey, doughy substance, which we optimistically call bread, spread very, very thinly with that same butter I got from the farmer. It is rather amusing to see how differently the girls deal with the tiny lump of butter we all have for the week. I put our lumps in ramekins, each with a different coloured flower painted on it. This is just as well, because Mary Jane spreads her bread as thickly as she can at the beginning of the week, while Elsbeth takes hardly any and looks forward to her last slice with all she has saved! And this is the way each day begins.

We are lucky though, compared to the people in the west of the country. I am so grateful that you are in that tiny farm, doing your Resistance work from there, right out in the country and not in one of the towns or cities in the West.

14

December 1944
Heerenstraat

Darling,

It is the end of yet another day without you, and the time when I can sit down and write to you. It was an unforgettable evening, two months ago, when we had once again climbed up into our loft, just before 8 o'clock. We are not allowed to have radios, let alone listen to them, but of course we all do. And without electricity, the only way we can make the radio work is by each one of us, strictly in turn, pedalling the stationary bicycle standing next to it. I have no idea how that makes the radio work, but it does. Every evening, at 8 o'clock, the BBC broadcasts to all the occupied nations and the opening words of their programme are: "This is London". To know that London is still there, for us is miraculous.

It was on the 17th September that we heard that the Dutch government in London had instructed the entire Dutch Railway to go on strike. Thirty thousand railway men answered that call and it meant that for some time the Germans could not move a single train. Going on strike entails the death penalty and some of the men were caught and shot, but by far the majority of them went into hiding. We are so full of admiration for them and it shows again what a deep and united love there is for our occupied country. (Yes, I know I am English, but I really feel I belong to this small and brave Holland more and more).

After a week or so the Germans found enough drivers from Germany to get trains moving again, but punishment for the strike was inevitable: from the end of September, all food transport to the West was stopped. How are these poor people going to cope?

And what about James!

My candle is almost burned out. I must leave the tiny stub for tomorrow, otherwise it is not fair on the girls. I so want to write down my feelings and fears about James, but it will have to wait until my next letter. I'll try and get some sleep.

Thank you for listening to me.
All my love, Isobel

December 1944
Heerenstraat

Darling,

Good news! Mary Jane has got hold of some fresh candles; they were a gift from one of the people in hiding to whom she brought a false identity card. She has no idea how on earth that person got hold of candles, and one doesn't ask questions about things like that.

I am so proud of her. She insisted a few months ago that she wanted to help the Resistance Movement by being a courier. Of course, she knows first hand what it is like to live in hiding as you do: to be forced to change your identity totally, to have to change your name into a false one and live at a secret address. You become a different person, and this means that the official identity card and ration card, which one has to carry at all times, is of no use at all, so false ones have to be printed.

You hear all kinds of stories about the way that is being done; I was told that some are even printed in England and secretly brought across the North Sea to the Dutch coast! How on earth do they do that? The beach from North to South is just flat sand, and these days it's covered in barbed wire, with a German soldier on watch every fifty metres. However, it is done, and when the youngsters receive the cards they hide them under their clothes and off they go on their bicycles to reach the people who are so desperate for them. I know this is dangerous work and I completely understand parents who won't allow their youngsters to take the risk, but

Sign on a Dutch beach during the war:

Danger Zone
You will be shot without warning

I can't stop our daughter; she so much wants to be involved, and in truth I don't even think I want to stop her.

So, I have just lit one of the new candles. Mary Jane has retired across the road for the night, Elsbeth is fast asleep and the whole house is quiet. I have lots of time for myself and I need it, because it is not just the war events I want to write down; there are other things that come crowding into my mind during the long, dark nights of this winter.

I want to write about James, our middle child whom we love so much but who is a source of constant anxiety. In all these years I have

17

never written down my feelings about James's birth and early years and it is doing me so much good to do just that. It hasn't always been easy to talk about it with you, especially as you would never believe it was as bad as it was and you kept on saying that all would be well. I know this was to protect and help me, but for me it is so important to 'relive' the story ...

He was born prematurely in 1932, weighing only four pounds but otherwise looking healthy. However, two days later he developed convulsions and we all thought he would not even survive. A specialist arrived late at night and prescribed a remedy to strengthen the baby's heart, which we believe saved his life, and although he continued to have convulsions, they gradually became fewer and less severe.

We started to think that James was quite normal, but as the months went by it became quite obvious that he was backward, very quiet and lethargic. The doctor kept saying there was nothing wrong, but my anxiety grew and grew and finally became an obsession. We visited a child specialist who was wonderful, and for the first time I felt that someone actually understood. She also suggested that I should see a psychiatrist. Oh, Jan Willem, I realise now what an awful time this was for you. You had to put up with all my worrying and you tried to put my mind at rest by reassuring me that there was nothing wrong with James, but that only made me think that you didn't care. Of course you cared, but you would not admit that to me or to anybody else. You were faced with the extra expense of my weekly train journey to Utrecht and then the costly visits to the psychiatrist, but you never complained and you only did what you thought would help me. You never told anybody anything about all of this: not your parents, or your sister and brothers, or any of our friends. So none of them ever knew the pain this psychiatrist caused us when he said, "My conclusion is that you suffer from a deep-rooted feeling of guilt because you left your parents who depended on you so much, and you went to live in another country. You could only overcome this feeling of guilt if you underwent some sort of tragedy, which would be a kind of compensation, or atonement. This 'tragedy' is in your mind and makes you think that your child is handicapped for life, although in the opinion of all concerned there is nothing really wrong with him".

When I came home and related all this, you were so angry. The visits to this man were stopped immediately and you told me over and over again how wrong he was. The sad thing is that I believed him and I still do. The fact that James is not normal is my fault. Although there were no more convulsions, James remained backward and at last it was recognised that there really was something wrong and that a mother's instinct had been right all along. By this time James was four years old, and he was becoming increasingly difficult, with outbursts of temper, and we desperately needed to find a solution.

Our doctor's wife, who had become a close friend of mine, told me that her husband sometimes had to make a professional call to attend children in a kind of holiday home somewhere in the woods nearby; the supervisor of this home, Miss Mulder, was a very kind and efficient young woman, who had training in the upbringing of children. It was suggested that James should attend the home for a few hours each morning and so meet and play with the other children. Something along these lines had been prescribed by a children's specialist, so we were delighted when Miss Mulder agreed to this plan. She was wonderful with him; she had a great sense of humour which he loved, and she was able to make him use his initiative, something totally new in James. It was all an indescribable relief for me because I was totally unable to manage our problem child – it was almost a miracle!

At the end of that summer the holiday home closed down. I was anxious all over again and you said that it would be all right – again. Well, this time you were perfectly right to be optimistic. Miss Mulder (we called her 'Sis' by this time) was going back to her parents in Rotterdam. We spoke with the child specialist again, who wondered if James could possibly go and live with Sis Mulder in Rotterdam for the time being. Looking back, I realise that everybody thought Sis's influence on him was a great deal better than mine – and they were right. Sis thought it was a brilliant idea! By this time she adored James, so he went to Rotterdam to live with her and her parents. Within days she became "Tante Sis" and they "Opa and Oma".

This was one of the most difficult times of my life, having to hand over my very special child to almost a complete stranger. Of course, it was agreed that James would visit us quite often and that we would go and see him in Rotterdam, and those visits were a great joy to us, but I had to share him. I have never told you what happened on one of my first visits there: James was standing on the steps leading to the front door and when I walked up with my arms wide open, he pushed me, hard. I almost lost my balance, but what was far worse was that he obviously wanted to push me out of his life.

When James was six, the age when Dutch children start school, it was decided that he couldn't possibly do that. It was then that Sis suggested that, with the help of books and advice from professional teachers, she could educate him. An excellent paediatrician was giving her support because he was very interested in James's case.

Learning to write and read was a slow process for James, but arithmetic was a huge success; from when he was tiny, he had always been interested in figures. When somebody looked at a picture book with him he was really only interested in the numbers on the pages. Pictures did not mean anything to him, either because he could not see them (it was discovered that he had very bad eyesight), or because he couldn't understand them. But he loved "doing sums!" When he was only five, somebody asked him, "What is five less seven?" After thinking for a tiny bit, he said, "Two nothings". "And now add six, James, what do you get?" The answer came at once, "Four". You and I were delighted and so proud of him, but we were told that concentrating on numbers and arithmetic was quite the wrong thing to do and that James would have to learn to become interested in the world around him.

Sis kept on believing in 'her James'. She noticed that he could play tiny tunes on the piano; nobody had taught him, he just did it. When she suggested that he should take piano lessons, people thought this was absurd – such a backward child, learning to play a musical instrument? That would never work! And her answer was, "James is not backward, he's only different from other children and his gift for music is one of those differences". I will never be able to thank her enough for that. Music has become the great love in James's life and has changed him into a much happier child. Whenever he is upset, or has had a convulsion, or is worried about something he can't achieve, the piano is the great friend he turns to.

And then the war began. We decided, with Sis, that it would be by far the best thing for James to remain in Rotterdam. We knew what was coming; we both understood that you would want to help your country and that this would mean working in the Resistance. There was no way in which we could cope both with this and with James at home. Of course, at the time we didn't know that we were going to be thrown out of our home and would have to find a roof over our heads. It would have been totally impossible and very unfair to ask Katja and Maurits to take James into their home as well as me and the girls. Thank God for Sis and for the haven James found in her.

December 1944
Heerenstraat

Darling Jan Willem,

It's going to be Christmas soon. In the past this was always a time of excitement, secret purchases and furtive wrapping; looking forward to the moment when you would find out what had been bought for you, or even better, to see the reaction of the person for whom you had found that one very special thing...

What special things can I get for the girls? And Darling, what can I get you and even if I did, how would I get it to you?

Jetje came last week and stayed all day. She is unbelievable, that cousin of yours. Unmarried, in a tiny flat in Amsterdam, doing some quite dangerous work for the Resistance... I have no idea what it is she does and she never breathes a word about it, and I wouldn't dare ask her, because you soon learn that asking even innocent questions can mean at best embarrassment, or at worst danger, for the person you're talking to. So we just talked about presents for the girls and, Jetje being Jetje, she had some wonderful ideas. For Mary Jane it's going to be some beautiful cotton fabric, just enough for a skirt, which Jetje still has in a suitcase in the loft above her flat. She assures me that she hadn't planned to do anything with it – something I have my doubts about! For Elsbeth, well, I feel ashamed not to have thought of something like this myself: some soft wool, also from this magic loft, for me to knit some new clothes for Elsbeth's beloved doll, Adriana.

Oh, that doll... it goes wherever Elsbeth goes. It gets carried around and sat down and picked up and talked to and sat down and picked up again all day long. And at bed time, Elsbeth tells Adriana stories. Perhaps I shouldn't, but sometimes I stand outside the bedroom and listen quietly to hear what those stories are about. She doesn't know I'm there; she thinks I'm downstairs with our one burning candle. Well, virtually every night, the stories Adriana hears are about you. Elsbeth tells her about the way that you can point out the stars in the night sky, each with its name and each with its meaning. She hears about the heroes of Greek and Roman mythology. The storyteller does not always get the names quite right, (well, she is only seven, and I'm sure Adriana doesn't notice), but Darling, the way she tells the stories you told her – she must have hung on to every word you said. Goodness, how she must be missing you.

Elsbeth
aged 6

What worries me, though, is that quite often the stories are about huge, happy families with lots of healthy, happy children. She obviously revels in thinking up names for everyone in her make-believe family and all the wonderful things they do together. Is it the fact that James is not normal? Is that frightening her? Is that why she's painting a picture of an impossibly happy, large family?

25th December 1944
Heerenstraat

My Darling,

Christmas day has come and gone. It was rather sad. Sad because we missed you, sad because it ended all wrong. I had been able, with a lot of queueing, to scramble together a rather nice dinner. It was so wonderful to see the girls enjoying every mouthful and every moment of this meal. And then, no more than twenty minutes after we finished, Mary Jane was violently sick. All I had struggled for was just thrown away.

Jan Willem, I was furious with her! I shouted at her, and blamed her for wasting all I had prepared! And now I feel so guilty. Poor sausage, it was not her fault; her stomach could not cope with all that sudden goodness. She's gone to her bedroom across the road and I want to tell her how much I love her and that I don't blame her, but now I have to wait until tomorrow. The curfew won't allow me to go and see her, and telling you what I feel now will never sound the same in the early morning light.

I heard Elsbeth in bed, telling Adriana all about a fantastic Christmas evening with a white tablecloth and napkins and silver knives and forks, with course after fabulous course, and nobody sick at all!

Do you remember that dinner party we had with Harriet and Pieter on the Queen's birthday in 1941? Nearly everything we ate was orange in honour of the House of Orange. You typed a menu for everyone on some old paper, and the typewriter you used was also pre-war, but it all looked great. I kept mine, and this is what it said:

MENU

In Honour of the Birthday of Queen Wilhelmina

31ˢᵗ August 1941

Soup: Julienne (named after Princess Juliana)
Salad with eggs (from Harriet, and quite likely illicit) and with bits of
orange
Meatballs in tomato sauce
Carrots, also orange
"Princesseboontjes" (what is known in English as green beans)
Victory Tart with apricots (also orange!)
Real coffee, brought by Pieter and nobody asked any questions
Champagne (ha ha) à la Jan Willem
Bordeaux Blanc (the very last bottles)

Something sweet – for the ladies, contributed by Pieter

Cigarettes – ten pre-war ones!

It was such a wonderful evening; it was amazing how much food we could still get hold of! Well, at the time things seemed pretty hard, but we had no idea what it was going to be like in this winter of '44. Do you remember, we sang the 'Wilhelmus', the Dutch national anthem? It must have sounded rather odd, because we had to sing it so very softly, because singing or playing it was, and still is, strictly forbidden, but to me it was the most moving rendition I have ever heard. And in the middle of the table stood the small picture of the Queen, the same photograph which sent you to the concentration camp two years later.

I have been looking through my hymn book, and especially the carols, humming a few to myself, remembering the many Christmas carol services I used to go to in England and the one broadcast from King's College, Cambridge, to which we always listened in Holland after we were married. How fantastic it would be to be there and hear again those wonderful words and tunes and sing with all the other people – in perfect freedom.

I came across the words of the hymn, "It Came upon a Midnight Clear" and some of them say exactly what everybody is feeling on this fifth Christmas under occupation:

> *And man, at war with man, hears not*
> *the love-song which they bring:*
> *O hush the noise, ye men of strife,*
> *And hear the angels sing.*

And:

> *For lo, the days are hastening on*
> *by prophet-bards foretold,*
> *when, with the ever-circling years*
> *comes round the age of gold;*
> *when peace shall over all the earth*
> *its ancient splendours fling,*
> *and the whole world give back the song*
> *which now the angels sing.*

I've learned these words by heart, so that I can think about them without the need of a candle.

All my love, Isobel.

December 1944
Heerenstraat

Darling,

We are coming to the end of 1944, and it's all becoming so frightening. Because they are realising more and more that they are starting to lose the war, the Germans are becoming nervous, angry and therefore crueller than ever; their *razzias* or raids are terrifying to watch. Somebody has told me that the Germans are now in such dire need of manpower that they're sending soldiers into streets, shooting warning shots into the air, and then rushing into houses, trying to find any men at all between the ages of sixteen and sixty. They drag them out and take them to God knows where.

I found Elsbeth at the living room window, watching what was going on, and seeing the father of one of her best friends being forced away like that. Jan Willem, what could I say? How could I help her? I just put my arm round her shoulders; we stood quite still, watching the now deserted street and then she said, "Let's pretend we are in church and then we can pray for him." I asked, "Can't we pray for him here, where we are?" She answered, "I think God hates to see this so much that he's gone home to church."

Darling, you sometimes come out of hiding to visit us for a very short time. Be careful. I only hope that you won't be here on one of the *razzia* days.

I am glad to know that God is with you all the time and doesn't run back "home" as Elsbeth believes, but how I wish this war was over and *you* could run home – for good!

Your Isobel

December 1944
Heerenstraat

Dearest Jan Willem,

Today is the last day of 1944. I am thinking of you in your tiny room in the small farm house where you are living with that brave farmer's widow, who is not only hiding you but also Louis and Betty, an elderly Jewish couple. Fortunately they are wealthy and are able to give a lot of money for their keep. That is just as well, because going out and earning money is impossible for them; they look very Jewish and have to keep inside all the time. It can't be easy for any of you being cooped up together; a great deal of tact and patience is necessary for that. I know my Jan Willem must have a bit of a problem with it … it's just as well that you're out a lot of the time, doing your Resistance work.

Other than members of the Resistance Movement, only I know what you do. Well, you really do two jobs: one is to collect money from various

28

sources that are willing to help the Resistance, and to distribute this money to people who have gone underground; in hiding they can earn no income with which to support their families. The other job is to find safe homes for Jewish children.

Jewish children lining up for deportation

Again and again, Jewish couples, who by now understand what great danger they are in, ask people to adopt their children so that, if their worst fears become reality, they will know that at least their children are safe. It is a very difficult task for you, because it is such a burdensome thing to ask of people: to take one, two or even sometimes three children into one's home is a very hard thing to do at any time, never mind the serious danger that this generosity would involve.

Travelling with a Jewish child needs planning. You have to make sure that any obvious Jewish features are hidden; large books to hide behind, or coats with wide hoods, are very useful on train journeys. Out on the street, it's great when it's raining – umbrellas give wonderful cover. Travelling with tiny children is the worst: they need to be read to, or entertained in other ways, constantly; otherwise they'll call for their mothers again and again. No wonder this particular job is nearly always done by women.

Even when a child is safely housed, problems can start. A neighbour might have spotted something, or a child of the family might, innocently, have talked to friends; whispers may have started in the neighbourhood and then the danger would be too great: the child would have to be moved.

I don't know what you find most frightening, travelling with a large amount of money, when at any moment you could be searched, or travelling with a Jewish child, when at any moment you could be denounced. Perhaps it's just as well you are not able to tell me each evening about everything that you do – I would panic, and that would not help you at all. All I can do is be proud of you.

Love you, Happy New Year,
Isobel

January 1945
Heerenstraat

My Darling,

Is this going to be the year of years? The year when it is all over? The year when it all ends: the darkness, the cold, the hunger and most of all, the fear?

It is the constant, overpowering, unrelenting fear that makes you want to curl up in a corner and hide under a thick, thick blanket.

It is the fear of the sound of those soldiers' boots on our streets; it is the fear of the sound of knocking, no, *banging* on doors in the middle of the night. It is a clever ploy, the midnight visit by the Gestapo or their friends. They smash their way in, trying to find Jewish occupants: they know people are tired and vulnerable when they're woken up suddenly and are frightened. When the soldiers suspect that people are being hidden, they test all the beds, even the spare ones, to see if the mattresses are warm, so that they know if they have recently been occupied. There is just no getting away from them.

And then there is the awful fear of never being completely able to trust anybody. Only the other day a story went round about a woman who had a very good friend who was hiding a couple of Jews. In total confidence this woman told someone – an acquaintance – about her friend, and probably they were saying to each other how much they admired her. The very next day this same acquaintance told the story to a small group of people. Well, among that group must have been a wrong pair of ears, because only hours later the friend and the Jewish couple were arrested and taken away.

I am so deeply grateful to Katja and Maurits who did not hesitate for a moment when we were thrown out of our lovely house in the Rozenlaan and immediately opened their front door for us. They have such a large family, two boys and three girls, and the youngest is only a baby, but they would not take no for an answer. The living room they gave us is small, but that does at least mean that the tiny stove heats most of it quite well. The bedroom is even smaller and Elsbeth's and my beds fit in there – just! I think that Mary Jane is quite pleased to sleep over the road, getting away from these tiny rooms and a small sister who quite often gets on her nerves. Eight years' difference in their ages is a lot.

The fact that I am so grateful to our wonderful friends makes me feel awful when I get irritated with the constant presence of a large family so very close by. Sharing the kitchen can be quite a problem and I often try to warm up our bits of food on the small stove in our living room. We have a small basin in the bedroom and we wash there. It's all a bit tight and there is only cold water, but at least we are independent.

Why did that S.S. Officer have to choose our house out of all the houses in town?

It is getting very late. More to talk about tomorrow. Thank you for listening – I'm sure you do. Your Isobel.

January 1945
Heerenstraat

Hello, my Jan Willem,

It is bitterly cold. Katja, bless her, got hold of a few more blankets, so we all three were given one and what a difference it makes! I have put mine around my shoulders while writing to you, so I will already be warm when I go upstairs.

And when I think of the lovely woollen blankets in our blanket box in our home... Most probably some Germans, living in our house, are making use of that luxury.

It was in the autumn of 1943 when our home in the Rozenlaan was taken ...everything seems to have happened in 1943: you were arrested in the spring and sent to Vught. Six weeks later you were released and I know you still think that it was thanks to a huge blunder in the camp's administration. Much, much earlier than we had hoped for, you came home. You looked dreadful: frightfully thin, emaciated, and with all your hair shorn off. I remember it frightened Elsbeth to see you like this and throughout the summer, when you were home with us, she was delighted with every centimetre of hair that grew again.

It was amazing how much the girls wanted to know about your life in Vught, but you were not able to talk about any of it, not even to me. What you *did* tell me, but not them, was the horrific feeling of total uncertainty. "What are they going to do with me? Send me to Germany or to Poland? Or shoot me right away? After all, we could hear the sound of executions day after day."

It took several months before you became stronger and more self-confident again. You loved to walk in the woods, just outside our back garden and you'd go there again and again. You knew them like the back of your hand, which is just as well because on 2nd October you received a very mysterious telephone call. It was from a Dutchman, who informed you that you were urgently required at the foundry in Vaassen, because you, he said, were the only one who knew the answers to various technical problems no one else could solve. You told him that you had been discharged from the foundry, but the man insisted, would not take no for an answer and said that a car was on the way to fetch you.

Those last few words put the fear of God in you: only a few weeks earlier we had heard the story about an acquaintance of ours, a medical doctor. He received a telephone call from a man who told him that a road accident had occurred and he, the doctor, was needed; a car would be sent to fetch him. The car did arrive, with three men in it. They shot him at his own front door. It was his poor wife who had warned us immediately.

October 2nd was Mary Jane's birthday, and this had obviously been discovered by these men and they reckoned, quite rightly, that you would be home to celebrate; birthdays are so important in this country.

You knew there was only one thing to do: off you ran into your beloved woods, where you hid for some time and then went to good friends of ours, where you stayed for a few days, just to make sure.

It was no more than half an hour later when a car stopped outside our house and four unpleasant-looking men got out and walked to our front door. Before we could stop her, Mary Jane ran to the door and opened it wide. The first thing one of these men said to her was, "It's your birthday to-day, isn't it? Are you having a lovely day?" It was as we had thought – they had chosen this day on purpose, and yet it was nonetheless hard to believe that minds can work like that.

It was your mother who came to the rescue – she had come for the birthday and she wasn't going to let anyone spoil the day. She strode forward with an almost regal look and kept the men talking and asking questions; she told them that she had no idea where her son was and that she had no explanation for his absence. On and on she kept the conversation going, giving you time to get away. After a while they gave up and walked back to their car, looking furious.

Unbeknown to them, while all this was going on I had contacted my neighbour and asked her to send her two small sons outside and make a note of the number plate. Our neighbour rang a friend, who knew somebody connected with the police, and he was able to confirm that this particular car had been requisitioned by the Nazis and had nothing to do with the company you used to work for.

If you had been less suspicious and had awaited the arrival of these guys, they would have killed you and there would be no sense now in writing down all my feelings and memories for you. Thank God for your reaction and thank God for your mother.

This type of murder is called "Silbertannen (Silver Fir) Murder." Several, probably many, good patriotic Dutchmen, who are known to the Germans to be anti-Nazi, are being executed in this way. These unspeakable collaborators betray their own countrymen like this, and I have been told that they 'earn' 100 guilders for each body…

Three days later you returned home and we celebrated Mary Jane's birthday without one German knowing anything about it. What happened had shaken you, had made you realise even more than before that justice no longer existed in our country and that you wanted to fight against the evil which had Holland in its grip. The very next day you joined the Resistance Movement.

We still don't know whether it was total coincidence, or if it was a deliberate reprisal, that only a month later our house was taken from us. The day before it was going to happen I received a message from a civil servant who worked in our town hall. He had seen the official piece of paper which would give a German officer the "right" to take possession of our house, and decided to warn us. That was a brave thing to do; he would have been in grave danger if he had been found out and it is a good example of the many ways in which resistance work is done. Sometimes great things are undertaken, sometimes much smaller ones, like this, but each one is a beam of light in the darkness in which our country is shrouded.

During the late afternoon and even into the curfew hours, friends and neighbours took away all of our most precious things on their bikes. I well remember Kees Jansen pedalling away with a carpet balanced on the back of his bike! It was such an important thing that they were doing: everybody knew that when the German officer and his men arrived, early in the morning, we would be given six hours to get out, taking only that which we were able to carry. All of those belongings are now hidden away in our friends' houses.

I still wonder if that German officer didn't think it strange to find such a calm mother and two daughters in a rather bare house, when he arrived the next morning. I am sure he must have suspected something, but what could he do? He was actually quite polite and apologetic. Was this yet another German who hated the whole thing? Are there perhaps many more of those than we realise? Well, whatever he secretly thought, out we went, and walking down the drive was like suffering bereavement.

Thanks to Katja and Maurits we had a home to go to. Because their house in the Heerenstraat is large, they were able to give us the rooms we live in now. Even so, given the size of their family it was a fantastic and generous thing to do.

Het Loo Palace

It is in a very important part of town, because quite close to our road is the Palace Het Loo, the house that Queen Wilhelmina used as her home until she had to flee her country at the beginning of the war. Standing in a beautiful park, the palace is special to me, because King William III and his Mary Stuart had it built in the 17ᵗʰ century.

Of course they lived in England, but they came to their beloved palace here as often as they could. Mary especially loved being here, so I am not the only British person who feels so at home in Holland. Is that why I feel this sadness, but even more, this anger inside me because of the brutal and totally unjust way in which this tiny land is being taken over?

This was a very long letter to you. I'd love to carry on, but I must stop, otherwise tomorrow is going to be impossible to get through.

Good night and God bless
Isobel

January 1945
Heerenstraat

Darling,

Disaster! Elsbeth has scarlet fever and I am terrified that the other children in the house will catch it. She is really very ill and the doctor has been several times. He has been marvellous and is taking such good care of her. Poor Mary Jane has of course been banned from the house altogether. Katja is most kind and understanding, and has given me some of her rations so that Elsbeth can have a few good things to eat.

Talking about food, I was in the garden yesterday and Katja's neighbour, Mrs Jansen, spoke to me over the fence. She had heard about the scarlet fever and offered me a peach!! She has several peach trees in her garden and keeps the fruit throughout the year in her cellar. Jan Willem, I didn't know what to do. Katja told us as soon as we moved in with her and Maurits that their neighbours were collaborators. Oh, in a very mild way, they just think that the Germans have got it right and that nobody should protest, but all the same... I wanted to refuse point blank, but then I thought how much Elsbeth needed fresh fruit like that peach and that people like them could prove to be dangerous if you anger them. I know that is cowardly in a way, but I have to protect you and your secret work and make sure that Katja and her family are safe. So the peach won.

Jetje came again for a day, and Elsbeth was really delighted to see her. They talked for ages upstairs in that cold little bedroom. Jetje is wonderful with children. It seems so unfair that she never married; she would have made a lovely mother. I remember her telling us, in strict confidence, that the only man she ever loved was married. They had an affair for some years, but then she felt this man was becoming very unhappy and very unsure of himself and Jetje being Jetje did not want him, his wife and his children to suffer a break up, so she ended it all. She never complained once, but we knew how very deep the pain was for her and I don't think for one moment that she'll ever get over him.

It must be her faith, her down-to-earth way of looking at things and especially her sense of humour that makes her so loved by everyone. Only she could have bought an ashtray with the inscription: "If the good God has not given you any children, the devil will give you nephews and nieces." And he has!

With three brothers, two sisters and lots of cousins all married and with families, she has dozens of them. They all adore coming to visit her in her Amsterdam flat, or being visited by her, and she is wonderful at giving each one the kind of attention he or she needs. Before the war she would take one of them to Paris or Brussels or Rome for an exciting weekend, no doubt showing them the wonders of those cities and having fun as well; she was always so clever at combining the two. Or she would take another of the children on the train to Haarlem or somewhere, having booked an hotel for the two of them in Amsterdam, then they'd travel back on the train and arrive at the station as if they were visiting there for the first time in their lives, and would have a spectacular weekend in that glorious city.

Archive image of Amsterdam Station,
where Jetje would arrive with the children.

Elsbeth later told me that they had talked about the ice flowers on the windows of our bedroom in the early morning, when they are on the inside as well as outside. To me they just prove how cold it is and that I don't want to get up and wash in the piercingly cold water in the basin, but Jetje told Elsbeth about the angels who paint those flowers during the night. During the dark hours, they put brilliant colours in their flowers, but we humans can only see the white of the frost when we wake up. Unless of course you look *very* hard and at the same time imagine the angels painting; then you will see tiny wisps of colour among the shapes of the flowers and so the bitterly cold early morning becomes a feast.

I wish I could think of things like that. I wish I could create magic for the girls and make this small world into which we are locked into one where moments of happiness come far more often for them. But I am not made that way – you have often told me that I am extremely clever at finding the negative side of things – not in people, never that, but in things that are happening around me. You also told me that you know why, and that some day I should write it down.

Well, I seem to be writing more and more and I promise, when I have plucked up an enormous amount of courage, I will use some of these evenings to do just that.

I bet you don't believe me!
Isobel

January 1945
Heerenstraat

The last few days have been a tiny bit milder and I have managed to cycle to Rotterdam to take some food to James, Sis and her parents. It seemed an endless ride. I didn't take Mary Jane with me this time; she is doing more than enough already and I often fear it is all too much for her. The tyres on my bike are now totally worn. You can't buy new ones; the Germans use all the rubber they can lay their hands on. Riding a bike virtually directly on the wheels does not make for an easy journey, especially one as long as this one: more than a hundred kilometres.

Katja was very worried and didn't think I should go. "You'll be away for three days; it is a very long journey, the cold weather might set in again and anyway, there is not that much food you can take all by yourself. Apart from the fact that you simply can't carry very much on one miserable bike, it's dangerous to be cycling along with a great amount – you're bound to be stopped by a German soldier. I will look after the girls, don't worry about that, it is *you* I am so concerned about. All that danger for a tiny bit of food for James?"

Bless her, she was totally right, but then it was not so much about food for James, it was that I wanted to see him again. With all that was going on, you would think that I could let go of James, knowing that he is looked after so well. But I can't. Loving your children is totally natural,

39

but your love for a disabled child is wrapped up in anxiety. You know they need just that little extra care and love because they miss so much in life. You worry, even when there is nothing you can do to help or change anything for them and you worry because you are the mother and you have this awful feeling of guilt.

Katja was right: it was a terrible journey. I was cold and hungry most of the time; I was terrified that I would get lost because of the possibility of missing signposts or, worse, whole roads not being there any longer, but people were very kind and whenever I was not sure there was always somebody who showed me the way. Halfway there I stayed the night with friends of Sis. It was wonderful to be with people I could trust, and they said they were very happy to have me with them on the way back. How do you thank people like that? They had a farming family not so far away, so the meals they provided were heaven. What is more, they had been able to get hold of some wood logs. How? Well, you just don't ask things like that, but to sit in front of a log fire… it's not really fair to make you envious!

I did reach James. Thank goodness he lives on the Eastern outskirts of the town, so I did not have to see the bombed out part, which was once its centre.

Rotterdam after German Bombing

It was unbelievable to see him again and he was terribly proud to show me the school work he does with Sis as his teacher. She really is wonderful with him, but it is very obvious that there is a great deal he won't ever be able to do.

There is one thing he is so very good at, however, and that is playing the piano. It was an absolute joy to hear him play small duets with Sis and he had even composed a tune! I *must* put out of my mind the fact that he had two bad epileptic fits while I was there. I know that it's my tension which starts them off and I do wish I could prevent it!

The journey back was much better. Relief I suppose, and knowing that I was on my way home again. Another delightful evening with Sis's friends helped as well, and the very cold weather we have had in the last few weeks did not come back during my cycle ride. If somebody in England, during my teens there, had told me that I would make this journey during a war and on a worn out bicycle, I would never have believed him.

All was well when I arrived home. Only one thing: Katja told me that Elsbeth had been informing her children in glowing terms that "her father had 'dived under', a term used for people who are in hiding, that he was living under water and that he had a table, chair and bed and that he was very happy". Katja was clearly worried, and quite right too; if Elsbeth goes around telling other people stories like that, we could all be in danger, you most of all. I had a long talk with her before I settled down to write to you. Don't worry, she was scared stiff, especially when Mary Jane had a go at her as well.

Take care, my dearest.
Your exhausted, but a little bit proud, Isobel

January 1945
Heerenstraat

My Darling,

I received your note, brought here by somebody I didn't know; he just pushed it through the door and then went off on his bike. Elsbeth was playing in the hall with the others and she picked it up.

When I read it I couldn't believe it: it says you are coming home for a whole day!! There is nothing that will make me happier. But Jan Willem, please be careful – you're on their black list, and I don't know how I would be able to bear it if you were caught because you wanted to visit me. And I can't even send this letter to warn you.

Mary Jane, wonderful, sensible Mary Jane, just laughed when I told her about my fear. She is so thrilled about your visit next week and she said, "Daddy knows exactly what to do, just enjoy the fact that he is coming".

She is quite right of course. Funnily enough, before your news arrived, I had planned to copy out an essay she wrote for her teacher the other day. We are so lucky that she stays with Johannes across the road, he being her Dutch Literature teacher. The schools have closed in this last year because the Germans are using the buildings, and there isn't enough coal to heat the classrooms anyway, so it's wonderful that Mary Jane gets private lessons from Johannes. Not very regularly, because also he is working for the Resistance and is sometimes away, but he sets her lots of work in as many subjects as he can manage.

Our eldest child doesn't always express her feelings, (certainly not as much as our youngest!), but I was quite moved by what she wrote in her essay:

"Feeling of Loneliness"

When I was a tiny child, I once lost my mother in the middle of Oxford Street in the large town of London. Then, for the first time I realised what it was like to be all by myself and I felt so lonely and forsaken, that I have never forgotten that feeling. Of course, my mother found me almost straight away and the sense of intense happiness, when she lifted me up in her arms, I will never forget either.

One dark winter evening, a few weeks ago, I was battling against a fierce snow storm, pedalling my deplorable bike. I could not see anything in front of me and my rear wheel kept on slipping through the layer of ice which was under the soft snow. That day I had to carry a large amount of money for the Resistance across the River IJssel and with difficulty I had managed it, somehow avoiding the German check points. I was now cycling home with a bag of rye and some butter. I was exhausted and my nerves were all on edge and again that feeling of desperate loneliness came over me, the feeling that everybody had left me.

Crying, worn out from tiredness, fear and nerves, I opened the door of our tiny living room. There it was, warmed by our tiny log stove and lit with the light of our precious candles. It was at that moment that I felt it again, this happiness of knowing that I was loved and that everything was all right.

I believe that each person knows moments in which he feels lonely, moments when he longs for a haven to which he can go with the problems and difficulties which have brought about his loneliness. There are two kinds of problems which can give you this feeling of loneliness. One consists of the kind you can't talk about with anybody and the other kind consists of the problems nobody can help you with.

I once read a story called "The Seventh Veil" in which it was said that every person has seven veils, covering his soul. For

43

people he hardly knows, he will lift the first veil, for slightly better acquaintances, the second, the third he will lift for those he feels more at home with, for his real friends he will lift the fourth, for the husband or wife, the fifth and perhaps even the sixth, but never the seventh. I believe this is true. Sometimes I have a problem or just a feeling I can't express, even to the people closest to me, and that gives me a horrible feeling of loneliness. I don't know what to do about it and it frightens me.

I remember when I was nine, not so long before the war, when a boy in our class became very ill suddenly and after a few weeks he died. We were all so little that it was difficult for us to comprehend this enormous happening. We all thought that our teacher would be able to help and explain; after all, she was grown up, she would know! But even she was lost and not able to help us at all. Then I felt so lonely again – I longed for someone I could run to who would be able to listen...

And now I am fifteen, and think of what my father told me. He would take me into the garden before this war had ever begun and show me the stars. He knew their names and spoke about them as if they were his friends. Not friends very close to you – after all, the stars are some distance away – but those you admire and are in awe of. And then he explained why the stars were so important to him, that they were always there, even when we can't see them during the day, they still are there. That we can't begin to understand them, that the mystery surrounding them is too great to take in. And yet, they are there, beautiful, serene, a guide to seamen and explorers, mysterious but also clear in their sparkling reality.

That, he said to me, is how we can think of God. Perhaps He shows us the stars to give a tiny indication of what He is. While our lives run happily along and all is light, we don't "see" Him all that much, but when it's dark in our world, He appears and guides us the way that the stars do.

He taught me a great deal that evening in the garden. What he said helped me so much then and it helps me now. All I need to do is look at the stars; it will remind me of the feeling of intense relief and happiness I had when, as that tiny girl, I found my mother again and in the same way, when a few weeks ago, I came out of the storm into our warm, safe living room. It will stop me from feeling lonely.

I was rather proud of our daughter when I finished reading this. Johannes gave her an 8 (out of 10) for it and wrote underneath, "Don't forget to pencil in your margins." Oh, the level headed Dutch!

It is getting really late and I should be going upstairs, but I know I won't sleep because I am both excited and frightened about you coming home. In your note you tell me that you love me so much that you have to come and see me again every so often. You don't even mention the fact that this could be dangerous.

Mary Jane's essay made me think of the time when she was a little girl. From the day she was born, we were so proud of her; she was a beautiful baby and toddler, very bright and with the deep sense of humour, inherited from you. When people said admiring things about her, we knew they meant it. We lived in Amsterdam at the time and were determined to do the 'modern' thing, so we sent her to the Montessori school there. She seemed to enjoy it immensely and we felt very proud of our decision. Then we had to move to a small village in Gelderland because of your new job, and we wondered how she was going to get on in the village school. The very first day she came dancing home, saying: "It is a lovely school – we all do the same things at the same time!" The Montessori System had been swept aside in one fell swoop.

And do you remember how she adored her class room teacher? Whatever "Miss" said, was Truth. I'll never forget when, one afternoon she came home from school, dying to tell us what had been happening. At the time, Princess Juliana was expecting her first baby any day. We were all very excited – the Dutch love their Royal Family – and not only was this going to be Juliana's first child, it was also going to be the first grandchild of our beloved Queen Wilhelmina. Obviously the teacher had been involving her class in the thrill of it all:

"Everybody must look out of the window now and then," she had said, "to see if you can catch a glimpse of the stork flying by on its way to the palace, carrying the little baby very carefully in its beak."

Well, all of the children, including Mary Jane, thought this absolutely wonderful and when we tried to tell her that this was not really the way babies were "delivered", she became furious; she stood there, stamping her foot and shouting that Miss had said so and that we knew nothing at all about it.

She was sure of herself then, and it has always stayed that way. Right through primary school, she earned brilliant marks and her teachers were convinced that she would pass the stiff entrance exam into the Gymnasium or Grammar School. Which reminds me, do you remember how my mother couldn't grasp the idea that in this country a Gymnasium is the most demanding secondary school and not a place where you do physical exercise? Language is a funny thing.

Mary Jane loved her life and was looking forward to the years ahead in which she would start her new school, begin new friendships and enter a whole new existence of learning, laughter and fun, when it all came to such a cruel halt. Although schools did carry on 'as normal' after the invasion in May 1940, already a terrible change had taken place. Nobody could trust anybody any longer and the teachers had to be very careful with what they said in the classroom. The ears of collaborators were on the alert everywhere and if a teacher said anything that could be construed as anti-Nazi, he or she would be removed immediately.

I am still trying to work out the mind of a collaborator. Is it *fear*, the same fear he felt at the time of the invasion, therefore it's safer to side with the occupier? Is it *bravado*, especially among the young ones? Is it *anger*? Anger at the way our country was being run and the thought that Hitler was doing much better things in Germany? It's difficult to say, and anyway there are such different degrees of collaboration. There is the turning away of the head when one sees something bad happen, right down to the betrayal of a person. It's difficult to know and I am so tired; I'll think about it again tomorrow.

"After all, tomorrow is another day," the very last sentence of 'Gone with the Wind'. *You* are usually the one who knows quotations, but this one I do remember. That wonderful book was written only a few years before the war and how we all enjoyed it! I do miss reading our books. I hope that whoever is in our house is careful with them…

God look after you on your journey here. I still can't believe you are coming.

All yours, Isobel

January 1945
Heerenstraat

Oh my darling, we so nearly lost you. I had a ghastly foreboding about this visit of yours, and I was right. Everything started fine: you arrived quite early in the morning, looking much better than I had expected. It was unbelievably wonderful to see you walk through our living room door. The girls took you over, as it were, and I had to be patient and wait. And then you took my hand, the way you always do with your fingers holding each finger of mine as if you want to tell a love story to each one, and then you let go and put your arms around me. I felt as though I had been on a long, lonely, dark journey, and I had come home again.

Then, you crazy idiot, you went out on your bike with Elsbeth on the back. She was so excited, waving to us as you rode off. She sat the wrong way round, naturally: you can see so much better what is going on around you, and it's much more fun than staring at a grown up back – all very important when you are seven years old.

You came home, both of you doubled up with laughter. At first it was difficult to understand what had happened, but then you told us: Elsbeth had stuck her tongue out at a German soldier!

I was so scared for a moment, that I could not react at all, but you were smiling away and saying, "Well there you are, even our younger daughter has done her bit for the Resistance!"

"But didn't he stop you?" I asked.

"Not an ordinary soldier," said Mary Jane quite calmly, "good thing it was not an officer, he might have wanted to look at your papers."

She was quite right and I told you there and then, with a few English swear words thrown in, that you were never, *never* to go out like that again. Mary Jane, who is totally bi-lingual, was dancing round the room, shouting: "Mummy, you told us never to say anything in English, because it's dangerous, that's what you said!"

"Yes," you laughed, "and that was *some* English." We all ended up laughing, not realizing what was going to happen just a few minutes later.

It was the sound of shooting that alerted us at first. Then Maurits, looking white as a sheet, came rushing into the room, warning us that another one of those dreadful *razzias* or raids was taking place in our street. It had started off with soldiers shooting some people at the corner as a warning – that had been the sounds we had heard. The soldiers would already have started raiding the first houses, dragging out any men they could find. Soon they would get to us.

It was Katja who organised us all; she always was the calm centre of any anxiety or frightening situation. You and Maurits wanted to run upstairs to your hiding place in the loft, but she, very sensibly, told you to go to the loo first! She then told me and the girls to go to her kitchen and that I should answer the door. She herself went out with her children; they have so many friends; it would be easy to go 'visiting'. It was a clever plan, because it would look as if I was the owner of the house and with my two young children it would look as if only one man could be hiding, not two husbands.

The hiding place in the loft was ingenious. A small catch in the panelling slid part of it open, and once someone had gone inside and fastened the catch it was impossible to see from the outside. There were lots of old chairs, tables and boxes in the loft, and Mary Jane went up with the men, moving a few chairs and boxes closer to the secret door once they had gone inside. I warned Elsbeth not to say a word to anybody – absolutely not a word. I trusted her totally; she is just as much involved with all that is going on as the grown ups.

Then there was nothing else to do but sit in the kitchen and wait. It was terribly quiet; I just stared out of the window, concentrating on the bare branches of a tree, not daring to look at the girls. It was almost a relief when we heard the pounding on the door. I went to answer it and a soldier walked in. He could only have been about eighteen – not that much older than Mary Jane. For one crazy moment I thought about *his* mother and what she was going through…

"Where is your husband?" he asked in German.

"In Germany" I replied.

Deep silence. He fingered a few things lying on the table and then, without another word, walked into the hall and up the stairs. Most hiding places were in lofts and the soldiers knew that all too well. I sat down again next to Mary Jane and just waited, clutching her hand. That awful, deep, foreboding silence had come back again.

Then we heard the sound of footsteps coming down the stairs. We looked at each other, hardly daring to listen, or to hope that it would only be one set of footsteps. It was! Oh, my darling, it was! The soldier walked straight out of the front door, ready to search another house, and we danced round the kitchen, laughing and crying all at once.

I turned to Elsbeth, wanting to praise her for keeping so quiet, but she calmly said: "When the soldier picked up that box of matches and put it down again, I thought, "What a stupid man, to look for my father under a box of matches!" I thought, "What a wonderful way to observe all this madness we live in."

Down you came, the two of you. Katja and her children came back and we had a party with all of our rations put together. And now you have gone again. It was such a short visit and it was broken into, but it was heaven to see you again. There was no time for you to read any of my "letters to you", but never mind, I'll keep on writing. Thank you for coming and thank you for your touch of a few moments.

With my love,   Isobel

January 1945
Heerenstraat

When you left, Darling, you told me how brave I was and that I was so full of self-confidence, something you had not seen in me before.

How wrong you were. Self-confidence was never there and I don't really think it is there now. You do extraordinary things during a war like this because you have to, and also perhaps because you are so incredibly angry with those soldiers daring to come into your country. But, self confidence? No, and you know as well as I do that the reason for that lies enmeshed in a story from long ago …

The whole of my life has been influenced by the fact that both my parents were stone deaf and therefore, as was usual in those days, never learned to speak. My mother was born that way and she became totally embittered with her burden, making life unbearable for every one around her as well as for herself. At birth my father's hearing was perfectly normal, but when he was eighteen months old his baby brother became terribly ill and, naturally enough, all the attention was directed towards him. An ear infection of my father's was, therefore, entirely neglected. It was discovered too late and he became totally deaf.

He never had a bitter moment in his life. Gentle, patient, full of fun – he was a marvellous conjurer – he had a tremendous sense of humour, loved doing things with his hands, enjoyed gardening, reading, tending his chickens and bees, drawing and painting. He won several prizes for photographs and helped to design the house in which we lived. He also enjoyed spoiling his wife (which did not help any of us much). Various close relatives joined together with help and advice, especially with regard to the upbringing and education of my older brother David and me.

This meant first of all that the poor boy, at the age of four, was sent to a prep boarding school. He was a year older than me, so I must have been tiny when he went off for the first time, but I well remember seeing him standing in the hall, head bowed, pretending to blow his nose. I knew better: he was wiping furiously at his tears. I adored him and I hated the grown ups for what they were doing. For years, term after term, we went through this hell.

Isobel as a young girl

I stayed at home with a governess; well actually, with one governess after the other. They were there to supervise my speech and behaviour, but apparently none of them stayed very long. Whether this was due to the fact that I was difficult, or that my mother was difficult, I do not know. If my mother treated any of those governesses the way she treated me, I can't blame them for leaving. Whatever I did, it was wrong. Unrelentingly she found fault with me, telling me that I looked awful, that I was clumsy, that I didn't try hard enough, pouring into me a feeling of such unworthiness that one day one of the servants found me standing at an upstairs open window, ready to jump. Self-confidence? I don't think so.

51

I loved it when I went to playschool. Doing things away from home was a revelation. Everything new was something to enjoy and to wonder at. The headmistress, Miss Merrington, wore an enormous hat pinned to her voluminous hair-do with large hat pins. She had some sort of 'tic' so that her head was always shaking, and I remember wondering when the enormous hat would fall to the ground – but it never did. One of the pupils was Martin Down; we always walked home together as we lived fairly close to one other. One day, and I will never forget it, he took me up a small hill and showed me how boys spend a penny. I was simply amazed, and ever so interested. Incredible really, how my parents kept things like that from me. Why did I never share a bath with David when we were toddlers, as should happen in normal families?

Things began to go badly wrong when I was in the High School, although school was not the problem, it was home.

Isobel at Croydon High Sc hool
(front right)

My parents, and especially my mother, came to depend more and more on my help. There was the interviewing of domestic staff – something that had to be done again and again because, like the governesses, members of staff gave in their notice at frequent intervals. I must have looked absurdly young to the housemaids and cooks who I was hoping would join our household. I felt so guilty when yet another member of staff had had enough and left. "After all," my mother would say, "you took her on, and it's your fault that she was the wrong choice."

My help was needed with shopping, with visits to the doctor or the dentist; I even had to accompany them on parents' evenings at school because of the translation and interpretation I had to give to anyone they 'spoke' to. It must have been very odd for the teachers having to tell them, through me, how well (or how not well) I had done!

Whenever visitors came, I had to be there in the drawing room, helping the conversation along. I had to answer the telephone every time it rang, and make calls for my parents. Although my schoolwork was important to me, I had hardly enough time to do it. Late at night, when at last nobody could interrupt me, I did as much as possible and those hours became the best for me. (Rather as it is now...)

It seemed so strange to me that during all this time my father couldn't see what was happening, that he did not notice how everything was piling up on top of me, that he did not realise how lonely I was and, most of all, that he did not recognise that my mother was becoming more and more difficult.

Then one evening, quite late, he came to my room to say good night and explained how mother had been closed in by walls of silence, able neither to hear nor to speak since early childhood. Those walls slowly became impregnated by fear, and then gradually by the bitterness which would alienate her from anyone near her, including her only daughter.

"But why", I asked, "does she not exclude you, and why is she not angry with you the way she is with me? Why am *I* outside those walls of hatred and bitterness and *you* seem to be happily invited inside?"

Then he told me about the special way they spoke to each other, through the language of signs. Of course I had grown up with the language of letters and vowels, formed by movements of the fingers and I was as fast in that, if not faster, than in writing. That was the way we 'talked'.

But that was not what he meant. Their language was one that had grown from such intimacy and understanding that they could communicate with each other using the tiniest of signs, nobody else in the room would have any idea of what had been going on between them. It was the only way they could totally understand each other and it was the only way my mother could be herself. In every other way she was unsure, and as a result she became embittered, always on the defensive. He told me how, as a young boy, he had met my mother at the special school for deaf children. He had been struck by her at once: tiny, very pretty and very, very vulnerable. And he, who had been neglected when he was so very young, saw in her someone he could care for and shield from any anxiety and hurt.

"I am lucky," my father explained, "I have been given a personality which enjoys everything that comes along; your poor mother did not receive that gift from the gods and that is why I want to help her through her deadly, silent life." Bless him; the fact that he also was living a life that was one of deadly silence did not seem to occur to him. I knew how much he loved me, but I also knew that his entire *raison d'être* was to help my mother, and at that moment I realised that he would never be able to prevent my mother folding round me, like a cape too heavy to shake off, the awful feeling of guilt. Whatever I did, something was wrong. My clothes were wrong, reading during the day was wrong, my posture was not correct and so on and so on.

I continue to wear that 'cape of guilt' and, darling, don't you know it! Despite all your love, all your assurances that I am really quite pretty and clever and that I choose exactly the right clothes and am kind and everything, I still feel unsure and guilty, and I can't stop it. I want to write more about those years, but I can hear Elsbeth in the room above; she sometimes has worrying dreams and I must go and be with her.

Love you, Isobel

January 1945
Heerenstraat

Jan Willem, I feel guilty. "What's new?" I hear you say. Well, when I went to bed last night and had managed to soothe and comfort Elsbeth, I lay there thinking about what I had written down. And then I remembered all the things my parents insisted I should learn, mostly those they would not have been able to do themselves.

They could never enjoy listening to music, going to the opera or the theatre; they could not go ballroom dancing or have fun watching one of the many musicals with their enchanting songs. The only type of theatre visit for them was the ballet – it was pure magic. To be able to follow the story that was danced to them in mime, the language they could so understand, was breath-taking every time. I remember going to ballets with them, putting my fingers in my ears, so that I could not hear the music, trying to see the ballet the way they were seeing it. It was terribly hard and quite soon I would let my ears fill with the music that is so much part of a ballet for those of us who don't live a life of silence.

So I was given piano lessons, singing lessons, elocution lessons, ballroom dancing lessons and ballet lessons. They would come to all the performances, glowing with pride, usually not able to understand very much of what was going on. I learned so much and I will never forget what they did for me in that way.

I am feeling guilty because I tend only to think about the hurt, and keep forgetting the kindness and thoughtfulness that was shown to me. And the awful thing is that I can't tell them that now, not by letter, not by finger language, not by smiling or embracing, because of the total impossibility of reaching them.

My love, Isobel

January 1945
Heerenstraat

Hello Darling,

Another Friday is over, and all is well. It is always the same. I tell myself not to be frightened, just to go and *do it*. Well, I do go and do it, but terrifying it is.

For the last four months now I have gone to the barracks in the town every week. Dutch political prisoners, both men and women, are being kept there in terrible conditions. You asked me if I would feel brave enough to visit your great friend Jan, who worked with you in the Resistance and who was arrested last year. You were very honest, told me about the dangers involved, but also told me that you were absolutely certain I could do this perfectly well.

Of course I said yes, so this morning I set off once again with clean underwear and a food parcel for him and was ready to fetch his dirty clothes. At the corner of the road I asked passers-by if it was safe to be on a bicycle today and they assured me that no Germans were grabbing them at the moment, so I started off along the slippery roads. There were several people waiting to hand in parcels for friends or relations. We waited about, stamping our feet to keep them warm. Why is this fifth winter of the war, with less food than ever and fewer and fewer ways to keep warm, the coldest of them all?

At last the gates were opened by the German guard and we all trooped in. We risked glancing out of the corners of our eyes, and could see a few faces glued to the barred windows of the cells. If we were to wave or even look at them openly, we would be sent away immediately, or perhaps even arrested ourselves.

Slowly we shuffled along, queueing in a long silent row. It is part of life under occupation: queueing for tiny bits of food, queueing to have your identity card checked, queueing to have your bags inspected and, worst of all, the ghastly queues of scared Jewish people, waiting to be pushed into open trucks and taken away to God knows where.

The woman in front of me told me that she was sure her husband would soon be released. "There must have been a mistake," she said, "I don't even know why they arrested him. He never took part in any Resistance work. The soldiers just came in the middle of the night and he had to go straight away. They wouldn't even let him say goodbye to the children." Then it was her turn to hand in her parcel. The German looked at the name on it and said that he was not there. "Where is he then?" asked the woman anxiously, "You *must* tell me where he is." "He is not here," yelled the German, "now get out of here or I'll arrest you, too." The woman went off, crying bitterly. Her story worried me; this had not been a case of a raid. Men who were taken in those were used for manpower in Germany or wherever else. Her husband had not been on a blacklist, nor was he wanted by the Germans. So what was this about?

Now it was my turn. I handed in the suitcase. The German guards all knew me, for I had been coming every week for the last four months.

You know, I often wonder during these visits, how these guards would behave if they knew I am English.

They opened my case and examined the clothes and food. I tried to look totally unconcerned, for in the seam of the pyjamas was some paper money and a tiny note giving the latest BBC news. The German picked up the pyjamas and my heart nearly stood still… it was all right, he closed the case again and carried it off.

When he came back with the dirty clothes, he warned me that the man had scurvy, which would mean disinfecting the clothes when I got home. Fortunately I had a little disinfectant, prised from a chemist after a lot of trouble.

On the way home I stopped behind a house and opened the case. I ran my hand along the seams of the pyjama trousers – yes, there was a note! I wormed it out and read it quickly. All was well with him except for the scurvy. He asked for matches – that was going to be difficult. However, I'd see what could be done.

When I got home I found Mary Jane and Sieneke, Katja's home help, doing a huge pile of washing. Laundries are a luxury of the past; everything has to be washed at home without soap and using the minimum of hot water. Sheets and underwear were draped about the room to dry. I felt so depressed and cold and hungry. What wouldn't I give for a cup of tea! But we haven't had tea for years now. I still have a little bit in the cupboard, but that is only used in cases of illness.

Sieneke, who is a refugee from Arnhem after the battle there, and whose sole possessions in the whole wide world are the clothes she is wearing, was telling us again the stories we never tire of hearing: what the British Paratroopers looked like – what they said and did and of all the wonderful things they had with them: real tea, marvellous biscuits, cigarettes and most astonishing of all: chocolate!

"And they were so kind and polite, even when the fighting was at its worst – we all loved them," Sieneke said. "And then the soldiers had to leave Arnhem, and soon after that the Germans came and threw hand grenades into the cellars of the houses as a punishment for the Battle of Arnhem and so we had to run and leave everything behind to be stolen or burnt by the Germans."

Poor Sieneke, she is so brave, never complaining about what has happened to her, just grateful that Katja and Maurits took her in and gave her the one little bit of space left in their house, in the shape of a tiny room, right up in the loft. And gosh, does she work for her keep! Up before anybody else, cleaning, scrubbing, chopping bits of wood into the tiny strips of kindling needed to get the little stoves going, preparing the meagre breakfast in such a way that it cheers everybody and doing anything she can to make life just that little bit happier for everyone.

I found her polishing the pewter jugs Katja keeps on the top of the large cupboard in her living room. Not easy to find polish for anything these days – but there Sieneke was, rubbing the pewter with a bit of raw leek, kept aside while preparing one of her magic soups (I have never seen anybody create dishes from virtually nothing the way she does).

She had been told by her mother, many years ago, that this was the way to polish pewter. Well, her mother had been quite right! The jugs gleamed in the sunshine slanting through the windows, reminding me of a 17th century Dutch painting, in which the light falls beautifully on a pewter vase.

I must remember what I learned. When all this is over and we are in our own house once more, we will be able to get our pewter plates and jugs from the hiding places where they are now. It will be such fun to practise what Sieneke was taught by her mother; my pewter will be gleaming and it will remind me of a very brave and special girl.

January 1945
Heerenstraat

My darling Jan Willem

I now know what became of the husband of the woman in front of me in the barracks the other day. It became clear yesterday, a day I would love to be able to forget, but know I never will.

It was a grey, still, very misty day, of the kind you only get in Holland. It must be something to do with the flatness of the country or the nearness of the sea or the permanent presence of water everywhere. The trees in the woods stood erect and silent, dripping with drops of mist. The clouds were low, deep, dark and impossible to penetrate; no Allied spitfires would be able to do any work on a day like this. The silence was eerie, and you could tell from the people moving quietly around that there was something threatening, that something deeply frightening was going to happen.

At about 4 o'clock in the afternoon Mary Jane walked into our living room. Actually, no, it wasn't walking it was *stumbling* and she looked dazed and more frightened than I had ever seen her.

"Whatever is the matter?" I asked her.

She fell into a chair and just stared and stared in front of her. She gave a little shudder, looked at me as if she had only just noticed I was there. Another little shudder and then she told me. She had been cycling with her friend Hannie, even though by this time the bikes were all in a deplorable state. It was tough going on worn out tyres or wooden or metal wheels, but cycling was, as always, a thing to be enjoyed. They had ridden for quite a few miles and were just passing through a wood on their way back, when they heard shouts. Lots of them. They stopped at once, wondering what to do. Should they go back or hide somewhere? And what was this about, what was happening? They were just about to go back the way they had come into the wood, when Hannie grabbed Mary Jane's shoulder and pointed.

In the wood, now silent, so still as if it was holding its breath, they saw a large group of men huddled together in a clearing and opposite them a row of German soldiers, ready with their guns. Without saying a word, without looking at each other, the two girls turned their bikes and cycled away, away from the sound of the shots which started at that very moment. Not wanting to hear and yet unable to stop hearing, tears streaming, they stumbled and swayed along the path between the silent, dripping trees – it was as if they, too, were crying. They cycled back in total silence. When they came to her house, Hannie looked back at Mary Jane, her face white and taut, and both of them knew they would never be able to forget what they had seen. Later that day I heard that 118 men had been taken to the woods to be shot as a reprisal for an attack on one German soldier.

That evening I kept Mary Jane with me after Elsbeth had gone to bed, so that we could talk and I could try to help her. How I wished you were here! I pretended you were with us and I imagined what you would have said. I think you would have talked about the evil that *has* to be fought against and that you are convinced that good will overcome evil in the end. You would stress that many people in Holland and in other countries are planning and struggling and fighting just for that. And you, with your deep faith, would have brought God into the conversation and made sure that she realised that in the end, it is only He whom we can ask

61

for guidance and help, not just for ourselves, but also for anybody in the Resistance, or anybody in the Allied forces and especially today, for the men Mary Jane had seen in the woods. It was well after 8 o'clock, after curfew time, when she and I slipped out into the dark so that I could make sure that she got safely across to her nightly home.

It was a strange day today. The weather had totally changed since our dreadful yesterday: the cold had come back and so had the sunshine. Everything was sparkling, and the trees looked as if they were decorated for Christmas. Each branch, down to the smallest twig, was encased in ice on which the sunshine was painting tiny rainbows. It looked incredibly beautiful. Through all that beauty, people were moving quietly about. Everybody knew what had happened, and virtually everyone knew at least one person or family who had been connected with the slaughter that had taken place in our village. You suddenly realised there were people missing: the son of the mayor, always about, always whistling; the elderly widower, a few houses down our road, who was forever trying to wheedle goods out of the shopkeepers; the son of the forest keeper, a boy, who, like his father, loved the woods. How on earth is his father going to keep doing his job, going into the very place where his son was murdered? The questions keep on piling up inside you and you can read them on the faces around you.

And then there are the whispers about the German soldier who was killed. Some say he was knifed, others that he was strangled. Apparently, he had been found behind a haystack near a farm. The German Commander had gone to the mayor and demanded that the man or men who had committed this crime should report to him. Nothing happened. Total silence. The Commander went once more to the mayor and told him that if nobody owned up, men would be taken as hostages and shot. Again, nothing happened, nobody owned up.

When it was all over, the wives or mothers received a polite little note from the Commander's office, saying that their husbands or sons had been executed. I won't sleep tonight.   Your Isobel

February 1945
Heerenstraat

Darling,

I needed cheering up, and it was Mary Jane who did it when she came across the road for breakfast. She told us that *every day* a woman opposite hangs her washing out in her garden, in sunshine *and* in rain. Why? Because, whatever else she puts out on her line, there were always three garments next to each other: one red, the next white and the next blue, the colours of the Dutch flag, the flag which is not allowed to be shown under any circumstances...

It reminded me of the story of one of our friends, who had knitted white socks for her five-year-old; along the very top she had added a minute red, white and blue edge. While walking with her daughter, a tall, distinguished gentleman approached. He gently lifted his hat, bowed slightly and said, "Madam, what delightful socks your daughter is wearing." She knew she had given him a pinprick of happiness.

When there are no pinpricks to be had and the evenings are lonely and dark and frightening, I go back, back to our lives before all this began and we were free and healthy and everything seemed possible.

After that wonderful year, when we were both in Woodbrooke, you persuaded your parents that you could study Mechanical Engineering at Birmingham University every bit as well as in Delft in Holland. It would broaden your outlook, you said. I am sure your parents knew very well that I had a lot to do with that outlook, but they agreed. You loved your time at an English university and ended up with a 1st Class Honours degree. I had followed a course in Social Work at Woodbrooke and when you started your studies in Birmingham, I began work as a social worker. In the meantime, David had taken over the care of, and responsibility for, our parents. That very understanding brother of mine had realised that I couldn't cope. He had always been a very calm person and could handle mother perfectly! He is extremely intelligent – not everybody becomes a Senior Wrangler at Cambridge – and has always been able to drift away to his world of knowledge, even while doing the things that have to be done for us lesser mortals. He was quite happy to work as Actuary for a Life Assurance firm in London, travelling back to our parents in Croydon every evening.

I became a working woman, having found a job with a firm of House Property Managers. My co-workers were all women and the aim was to combine a successful business project with an improvement in the living conditions in the property to be managed. It was owned by the Church of England and consisted of ugly blocks of flats in Islington and Southwark – this was the early twenties, and they were slums. My job was to collect the rents. Doing this, I came to know the tenants and to understand their problems and difficulties. I visited each of my districts once a week, collecting the rents and making notes of all the complaints. There were quite a few of these, one of the most frequent being blocked-up WCs, and no wonder: there was only one of these on each floor and each had to serve five families.

So much has happened since then, and yet it's all there, still fresh in my mind. It was quite rough and even scary during some of the days, but what none of us appreciated at the time – and why would we – was the fact that you could discuss anything with anybody in perfect freedom, a 'privilege' that's not possible now.

God keep you safe,
All my love, Isobel

February 1945
Heerenstraat

It has been a good day, Darling.   Both girls went out with their friends to fetch pans from elderly neighbours, put them on a rather wonky trolley and then off they went to the soup kitchen. We all receive a few ladles of soup from there. Well, soup… it's a rather watery substance with a few black potatoes floating on the top, but we eat every single drop. The girls even put their plates on their side to scrape the last few drops off onto their spoon. Not polite, but very understandable.

Actually, today the soup was rather good! There were some tiny bits of something that looked a bit like sausage in it. It made our day!

It is evening once more. The curfew makes everything outside deadly quiet and the blackout paper curtains cut out any noise anyway. So I'm going back again to London and my job….

If the tenant was unable to pay the rent, my job was to find out, with tact and patience, the cause of this failure. Everything was noted down and reported back to head office, then an attempt was made to find a remedy for the problem, which was the positive side of our work. My co-workers were all considerably older than I was, and so were able to give advice and help, which I, not being experienced at all, was unable to do. This could be a bit depressing sometimes, but on the whole I really enjoyed the work and got on well with many of the tenants.

It was surprising how many of the women in the flats managed to keep their house clean and attractive in spite of poverty and large families. But there were also many cases where things were very different. Often, trouble was caused by drink, addiction to betting or by unemployment and in these cases the tenant was always behind with the rent.

Our boss was a fierce looking lady called Mrs Lee, who was scared of no one. I remember one occasion when I returned to the office with the report of yet another failure to pay the rent. I had been told a pathetic story of poverty, too many mouths to feed, ending up with "and now I'm expecting again." When I informed Mrs Lee of this (you never *told* her anything, you *informed* her), she leapt up from behind her desk, pinned her hat firmly upon her head, threw on the feather boa which she always wore round her neck and marched out of the office saying: "I'm going to have a few words with the husband." The population of this world would be greatly reduced if it were up to Mrs Lee.

Only once was I really frightened during the years that I did that job. I was coming down the stairs in one of the buildings in Islington when I heard lots of running footsteps behind me. Before I could turn round I was grabbed from behind, pushed to the ground and four boys of about eighteen rushed off with my bag. It contained all the rent money which I had collected that morning: £30 – quite an amount in those days. They ran back upstairs and then across the flat roof. There was no way in which I would even have been able to follow them, let alone get that bag back, so I drooped back to the office, not daring to think what Mrs Lee would say.

She was fantastic. She gave me tea with a disgusting amount of sugar in it, told me not to worry about a thing and rang the police. They traced those boys in no time and a court case followed in which I was obliged to give evidence, which I did not like one bit. Facing those four was very strange; I thought I was going to hate them, but I couldn't help feeling sorry for them. They seemed much younger and smaller than when they stormed down those stairs towards me, and they looked very scared. Was this fear there only for that day, or had it been inside them for years, ingrained because of a brutal father or fighting parents? I wasn't sure, but I realised that during that morning in court I was taking a profound step in my career as a Social Worker.

I had been desperately frightened at the time; I thought nothing would ever scare me again, but how wrong I was. One ghastly fright is very different from the ever present fear that has been around us for such a long time. And it goes on. You think it can't get any worse and then you hear about a couple of Jews discovered one night. How? Because the Germans, searching for their prey, crashed into the house in the middle of the night, ordered everyone out of their beds and then felt all the mattresses to see if any "spare beds" were warm. If they were, they knew they were on the right track and of course they found what they were looking for. The Jews were taken and so were the brave people who had hidden them for months and months. Awful. And even worse is that someone had betrayed them.

The candle is very, very low; I'll blow it out so that there's enough for tomorrow night, then go upstairs and think of you.

Your Isobel

February 1945
Heerenstraat

My darling Jan Willem,

Your mother was here today – she really is wonderful. Elsbeth especially adores her and thinks that whatever her grandmother does is perfect. She told me this afternoon, "You know, when Oma wants to turn a page in her bible she blows at it, and it works!" Indeed, the pages of your mother's bible are so wafer thin that the blowing method is best. To Elsbeth it is pure magic. It's a beautiful, small bible that she's had for years. I think it is incredible, the way she reads a part of a chapter every day, putting a little mark with her pen or pencil where she has reached and whenever she has finished both the Old and the New Testaments, she starts all over again. She must know all the names and all the stories better than anyone.

She let me read it today and it was fascinating to see little comments and notes in her beautiful handwriting on many pages. The German invasion was during the second book of Samuel; Hans, your older brother, went into the Resistance Movement not long after that and this fact was written down on a page in the first book of Kings. Several times, beside verses in which it says that God will rescue the Good from the Evil, she has placed exclamation marks.

I came across the last few verses of the prophet Amos towards the end of the Old Testament. Amos is prophesying the return of the people of Israel from their exile and says:

"God promises that the day is coming when new wine will drip from the mountains and flow from all the hills.
I will bring back my exiled people and they will rebuild the ruined cities and live in them;
They will plant vineyards and drink their wine;
They will make gardens and eat their fruit;
They will be in their own land once more and it will not be grasped from them ever again."

Above it, right across the page was written in her own handwriting the anguished words, "O! Nederland", and next to it the date: 4 - 9 - 44.

O! Nederland OBADJA 4 - 9 - 44 849

Belofte eener heerlijke toekomst.

11 Te dien dage zal Ik de vervallen hut Davids weder oprichten, en Ik zal hare reten dicht maken, en wat aan haar is afgebroken, weder oprichten, en zal ze bouwen als *in* de dagen van ouds;
12 opdat zij erfelijk bezitten het overblijfsel van Edom, en al de heidenen, die naar mijnen Naam genoemd worden, spreekt de Heere, die dit doet.
13 Zie, de dagen komen, spreekt de Heere, dat de ploeger den maaier en de druiventreder den zaadzaaier

genaken zal, en de bergen zullen van zoeten wijn druipen en al de heuvelen zullen smelten;
14 en Ik zal de gevangenis mijns volks Israëls wenden, en zij zullen de verwoeste steden herbouwen en bewonen, en wijngaarden planten en derzelver wijn drinken, en zij zullen hoven maken en derzelver vrucht eten;
15 en Ik zal ze in hun land planten, en zij zullen niet meer worden uitgerukt uit hun land, dat Ik hun gegeven heb, zegt de Heere, uw God.

vs. 11: Hand. 15:16, 17.

DE PROFEET OBADJA

Profetie over den ondergang van Edom en de verlossing van Israël.

Het gezicht van Obadja. Alzoo zegt de Heere Heere van Edom: Wij hebben een gerucht gehoord van den Heere, en daar is een

10 Om het geweld, begaan aan uwen broeder Jakob, zal schaamte u bedekken, en gij zult uitgeroeid worden in eeuwigheid.
11 Ten dage als gij tegenover *hem* stondt, ten dage als de uitlanders zijn heir gevangen voerden, en de

68

September 1944 – this, of all the months of the war, was the one of highest hopes and deepest disappointments. Paris had been liberated and on September 3rd the English were in Brussels. The very next day Antwerp was liberated. The BBC and our own secret Radio Oranje were telling us that, "the hour of liberation is very close." Queen Wilhelmina, in one of her nightly broadcasts, said, "You know that your liberation is at your doorstep." But then at Arnhem everything went wrong: so many airborne troops killed, so many Allied soldiers becoming prisoners of war.

British paratroopers land in the Netherlands during Operation Market Garden.

And poor Arnhem; Sieneke told us that the inhabitants fled an empty, devastated town and the Germans pillaged whatever was left behind. I wonder whether some day, when this is all over and we live in peace again, there will be a beautiful cemetery near Arnhem to commemorate and honour all those soldiers who died. Now, five months later, when I'm cycling to Rotterdam again to visit James and bring some food to him, it's weird to know that south of me, not all that far away on the other side of the rivers, is a free part of Holland where there is no longer the fear and despair which still penetrate everything here.

Forever yours,
Isobel

February 1945
Heerenstraat,

You've been home again! You simply arrived, yesterday afternoon, and stayed until late this morning; it was right of you not to let us know beforehand, because I didn't have to go through all the worry during your journey. It was a glorious day, although still cold, but the sun was shining and we found some snowdrops in the garden.

"The next time those brave and beautiful flowers come up, we will be free," you said. You are totally convinced of that, and I do so want to believe it too.

Katja had scrambled a lovely meal together and we ate in their dining room, having a wonderful time with the two families round their big table. We played games and after that it was decided that the little ones should go to bed and the others go into the loft to hear the BBC news.

Well, one little person did not go to bed straight away – Elsbeth walked with you into the garden and in the darkness you both saw a V1 flying across the sky. She asked you what it was and you told her – that it was a ghastly weapon on its way to England, something that was going to destroy lots of houses and kill lots of people and that both of you, standing there and watching it go, could do absolutely nothing to stop it.

The sinister silhouette
of a V1 bomb
over a residential area

"But," asked Elsbeth, "what about the pilot?" You told her that there was no pilot; that this evil thing was making its dreadful journey all by itself. You then told a very subdued small girl what the word V1 meant; with your enquiring mind you always want to explain everything, even to the smallest size audience, and in this case very young as well. You told her that it stood for *Vergeltungswaffe* or *Weapon of Revenge*. "Why revenge?" she asked, and then you tried to explain that the Germans were angry with the British because the British were angry with the Germans – for occupying our country and many other countries as well. It must all be very bewildering for a seven year old. She is still so young that I think she will not remember much about the years she is living through now, but standing in the garden with you last night, watching this V1 moving across the sky – I wouldn't be surprised if that is one of the things that will leave a deep impression on her and will stay with her for many years to come. It was so good to say good night to her together and see her fall asleep so happy, just because she knew you were there.

The night in the single bed was cramped, but it was heaven! Then, this morning, you had to leave again. When you kissed me goodbye, you whispered, "Look under your pillow when I have gone." So, when the long and stormy farewells of the girls were over and you had left, I immediately ran upstairs and there found a thick envelope. On it was written in your hand-writing, "To Isobel, to read by candlelight". The evening seemed to drag and drag. I had never looked forward so much to putting the girls to bed and lighting that candle. Inside the envelope were two pieces of wood, fastened together with three old curtain rings. On the front you had painted the names and numbers of the first six months of the year, with two daffodils painted at the side. The back held the other six months, with fuchsias as decoration. The names and numbers were painted in deep red, apart from everybody's birthday; they were in soft pink, as were Christmas Day and May 10th, the day of the beginning of the war. Inside, in gothic letters in red and blue, was a poem that you had written, about us and about James.

When I would shut life's
granite facts from sight
living in idle dreams, and
thus forsake
my task and talents, you
bade me awake
and showed to me the battles
I must fight.

And when life led us on
into the night,
and made you suffer for a
sweet boy's sake,
you often leant on me, with
me to take
the road of faith from grief
towards the light.

All this, and heaven too:
no sunshine charms
like sunshine breaking
through a clouded sky,
and happiness shines brightest
after sorrow.

So one warm night twixt
lonely eve and morrow,
we enter timeless heaven,
you and I,
our heaven, beloved, in
each other's arms.

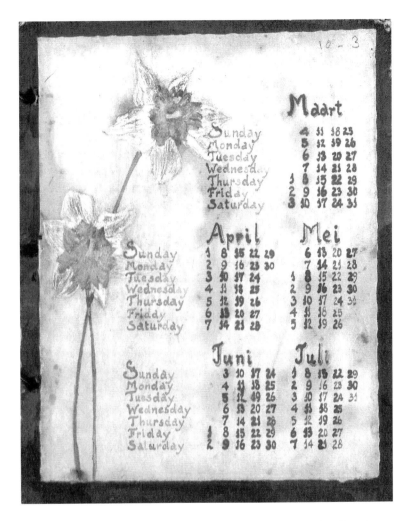

I will keep this little wooden book somewhere nearby for always.

February 1945
Heerenstraat

I lay in bed last night thinking about the words you had written in

73

your poem and looking forward to the daylight in which I could reread them, and I was reminded of the Woodbrooke days when you were trying to teach me your language by reciting Dutch poems to me. I found it a rather advanced introduction, but I remember enjoying the beautiful sounds and rhythm of the words and I am sure it was a great start towards learning your quite difficult language. I encouraged you to start writing poetry in English and I remember very well going to church with you and my parents in the beginning of January. You noticed the four large candles, unlit but all previously burned to a different height, and asked me the reason for them. I explained that during each of the four Advent services a new candle was lit, bringing the light towards Christmas. You were very quiet on the way home and that evening you wrote your "January" poem:

The Advent candles in the church
At their four different heights,
Stand now blown out,
There's no more need to burn:
The Christmas scene has gone,
The shepherds left some time ago.
But on Twelfth Night the magi with their gifts
Of gold and myrrh and frankincense arrived
And gave this month the title of Epiphany.
Through snow and frost,
Through slightly milder days,
This first month of the year
Will proudly bear that name
And, at its end,
Will leave the month that follows
The first few snowdrops as its dying gift.

You let me read it the next day and I was moved by the way you expressed the whole feeling of the first month of the year, as well as the atmosphere of an Anglican church. You have always been able to do this: cross the threshold of any building and feel and *understand* it. It is the same with religions: you study them, you respect them, you try to understand them and, with your tolerant Quaker mind, you very often do.

It took me much longer to find my way. Both you and I had been much impressed by the Quakers we met in Woodbrooke, so much so that we decided to become members. After our marriage we organised a Quaker meeting to take place every Sunday in our flat; it was to become the very beginning of the Quaker movement or "Society of Friends" in Holland. I admired the Quakers and was happy for you to have found everything you needed there, but all the time I felt the need for more spiritual support and guidance and started to attend the services at the "Doopsgezinden", or Baptist Church.

I felt quite guilty about jumping from one church group to another and spoke to the Baptist priest about my worries. This is what he said: "To me the different churches and religious groups are like a street with different houses. Each house has a family and each family has its own way of doing things and its own traditions. But it is still one street. There is nothing wrong with visiting other families in the street and learning from them, even being taken into their home. In an ideal world, there is still the one street, with families respecting each other's households."

So this is what we did; we 'visited each other's houses'. I often enjoyed the calm of quietness and prayer during a Quaker meeting in our flat and you came with me to the Baptist church with its simple service and its thought-provoking sermons, like the one we listened to one Sunday in the spring of the year James was born.

I asked Dominee van Laren if I could have a copy and he brought it to our house. I have kept it all these years and I read it again to-night. This is what it said:

Jeremiah 31 verse 9: I will guide them to streams of water on a smooth road where they will not stumble.

The church calendar is like a road winding itself through the year. Last Thursday was Ascension Day and so now we are walking the bit of road called Ascension Tide: the ten days between Ascension and Whitsun Eve.

Ascension Day, or Holy Thursday, is when we commemorate the ascent of Jesus from earth to heaven. What, however does it mean? When I looked up the word Ascension in one of my bible handbooks, the index gave several page numbers where text references were given and then it said: photograph.

Well, that should be most interesting and not a little helpful!

When I turned to the page, I realised what it was: a photograph of a church, built on the Mount of Olives, commemorating the Ascension. For the apostles it must have been a most bewildering event. As if what had happened forty days earlier was not enough, their Lord was now leaving them again and from now on they would have to walk their road alone.

But He did give them a promise: the Holy Spirit would come and give them an inner strength and joy to help them on the way Jesus had asked them to go.

We are all walking our bits of road. Sometimes they are the steep bits, where we can't see anything but the incline; sometimes there are marvellous straight stretches with a clear sky and with signposts telling us where to go.

There are those bits of road when we think we are of no use to anybody or we think somebody else we see walking along is much cleverer, or has much more confidence.

And you think to yourself: I must try and be like him or follow the road exactly the way she does.

But as Rabbi Martin Buber says: "God created you to be you and to walk the road your way."

God teaches us that people are not alike and should not try to be alike. With the creation of each person, something new has been brought into the world that was never there before. Every person is a new "appearance" on this earth and it is that person's task to fulfil his talents; it is not his task to repeat what somebody else, however great, has already done.

And how do we do that? Talking about it and listening to it here in church, one thinks: yes, that is the way I am going to do it – all week long. And before the end of one day, let alone one week, one has slithered into a side road, struggling among the thorns and nettles we grow around ourselves by worry, jealousy and dissatisfaction.

Those are the bits of road where God does not seem to be around at all, rather like the road the apostles had to walk between Ascension and Whitsun. But there was that promise. At Ascension, the cloud that eventually hid Jesus from view symbolises the presence of God and of His Holy Spirit, that Spirit which pierces every cloud on our road.

It was good to read it again tonight. I wonder how Dominee van Laren is now. Is he still preaching? Is he still able to hold his services in his beloved church in that small town where we lived, in the west of the country? He was never afraid to speak the truth; he hated any injustice and would never have bowed down to the Nazi way of thinking.

Has any collaborator sat quietly at the back of the church, listening, not moving a muscle in his face, but taking in every single word, or even nuance, during the sermon? If van Laren is still preaching, I certainly hope he is not quoting Martin Buber...

You admire Martin Buber too; you were much affected by this Austrian born Jewish religious philosopher's book "I and Thou", in which he describes his faith in the form of a discussion between man and God. It is one of those very depressing thoughts that under this régime many deeply talented Jewish minds have been wiped out as if they never existed. I know what you would say to this thought: those deeply talented minds will live on, whatever Hitler and his friends might dictate. We will carry them on; we will make sure they are *never* wiped out.

You are right.
Love you,   Isobel

February 1945
Heerenstraat

Darling,

Another day has passed, and I wish I could be with you tonight. I know you will be feeling very upset, angry and helpless because by now you will have heard the story about Frans van der Weerd and what happened to him and many of his friends today; important news stories like that race round the whole of the Resistance Movement.

Only this afternoon our very good friend Marjolein came to tell me – she arrived looking as white as a sheet. I know how brave Marjolein is: after all, she works in the Resistance, but even she has been thoroughly shocked. To begin with she just stared at the wall, tried to talk, and then just stared again. I waited, knowing that I needed to be patient, but God, was I worried. I was sure she had come to tell me you had been arrested.

And then the story came out. Frans, one of the highest chaps in the Resistance Movement, had been arrested a few days ago. He had his diary on him, and of course the Germans who interrogated him looked at it. At today's date it said, "LG no.15 – 2 o'clock". They must have asked him what that meant – and he told them. He admitted that members of the Resistance Movement were going to meet at number fifteen Leidsche Gracht, one of the most beautiful canal streets in Amsterdam, starting at 2 o'clock.

This was to be no ordinary meeting: it involved the very top of the Resistance hierarchy and a great many people were going to be there.

He must have been convinced that as soon as the word had gone round that he had been arrested, the first thing that would happen was that the intended meeting would be moved to another date or venue, or even both. Well, something went terribly wrong: nothing was changed and this afternoon, when dozens of people came together for their meeting, the Germans were waiting.

Leidsche Gracht today

Marjolein's sister, Ester, who lives in Amsterdam and is one of the most important women in this group, should have been there but had been delayed, and as she came racing round the corner on her bike she saw, to her horror, all those friends with whom she had worked for years being herded into official cars by the soldiers.

All she could do was turn round her bike and ride away. Bent over the handlebars, hardly able to see the cobble stones through the tears streaming down her face, she got home, grabbed some clothes and other belongings and went straight to a friend's home. Staying in her own house would have been madness; it would not be long before the Gestapo would have forced her name and address out of one or more of the newly arrested people. From the relative safety of her friend's home she was able to tell the terrible news to as many Resistance workers as she could, including Marjolein.

I know how fond you are of Frans; you met him when your brother Hans took you to your first meeting and you were immediately impressed with the way he handled the meeting with calm assurance, setting out plans for the coming days. He was a finance man, involved with the NSF, or National Support Fund, organised by the Dutch government in London. His task was to oversee the distribution of money to the various branches

79

of the Resistance: the people printing illegal papers or false identity cards; people like the train drivers who had gone on strike and did not get paid any longer and could not provide for their families; the many people who were harbouring Jews or Resistance workers. Then there were those looking after Allied soldiers or airmen who needed to be spirited away from danger. You told me that you would never forget the way he quite light-heartedly asked you, "Are you joining us in our game?" And you replied that yes, you were joining.

I remember you describing your train journeys to deliver money to various people. You had been given your new identity and had rehearsed your false name many times, so that you would say it automatically if you were stopped and asked. Inside the organisation you knew each other only by your assumed names, and of course you had no idea of each other's addresses, nor did you know anything else about one another. You once told me that when you sat and talked to someone to whom you had brought money, you thought to yourself, "This person opposite me has absolutely no idea who I am."

Yet, under those strange circumstances, friendships grew. There was that wonderful woman in Winterswijk, who was cheerfully – genuinely cheerfully – hiding three small Jewish children whom you had not been able to visit for a few months. She was utterly delighted when you knocked on her door again; she had been convinced that you had been caught.

I also remember you telling me about what you called, "a rather unpleasant quarter of an hour". Well, I would have put it a bit stronger. You were sitting in a train to Utrecht in a third class compartment. The two wooden benches, which sat five people facing each other, were fully occupied. There was a rather stilted conversation going on, punctuated by eerie silences; everybody knew that German soldiers were moving from one end of the train to the other, checking travellers' papers.

You knew that 'yours' were all right, although they were not yours at all of course – they used to belong to a slightly older man who had died some time ago. This is called "having a corpse behind you." Now your photograph, not his, was in place, put there by the magic men who created the false identity cards. You were rehearsing yet again 'your' name, plus your date and place of birth; you had to be sure you would be able to say it all without any hesitation.

It is very hard to know what one's most natural attitude should be at a moment like this, when a soldier in the detested German uniform slides open the compartment door and walks in. You must not draw attention to yourself by interfering with whatever is said between the soldier and any of the other passengers, yet not to show any interest whatsoever can be equally risky.

In the event, the soldier inspected everyone's papers quite thoroughly, enquired about some innocent parcels on the luggage rack and then, quite abruptly, left. Immediately, excited talk began; not the safest thing to do, you thought. It is only a small percentage of Dutch people who collaborate with the Germans, but even a tiny percentage still means quite a few people... All went well, however. Had you been searched, they would have found 40,000 guilders.

I am so deeply sad about Frans and all his friends and colleagues. You must be suffering and there is nothing I can do.

My love, Darling
Isobel

February 1945
Heerenstraat

Dearest Jan Willem,

It is almost the end of the month. Strange, it is the shortest one of the year and yet it seems to have gone on, and on, and on. It's the long dark evenings and mornings that make it seem endless. Well, at least it offers plenty of time for thinking and remembering.

I was darning, yet again, the girls' socks the other day, using the darning 'egg' in the shape of a mushroom – you remember that one? Bright red with white spots. It used to belong to your mother, but she gave it to me in despair, because every time she went to use it when she was visiting us, it had disappeared! During the second year of the war, we were still in our own house in the Rozenlaan and Elsbeth was just four years old. Even then she knew exactly what was right and what was wrong, and a mushroom in a darning basket was simply *wrong*. The first time the thing went missing, we searched and searched and simply could not understand what had happened to it. We never thought of asking a four year old if she had seen it, but we should have done: she had taken it into the end of the back garden, where she had 'planted' it among the trees. *That* is where a mushroom belongs. She kept on doing this, taking it to a different part of the garden every time, even going through the gate into the wood behind and virtually burying it there. She doesn't do it any more, partly because we don't have a garden ending in a wood here, but also because she is growing up and the magic she believed in is slowly disappearing.

All my love,
Isobel

March 1945
Heerenstraat

February has gone and today is my birthday. I told the girls I was born in a leap year, (to them 1904 seemed an incredibly long time ago) and that my birthday might easily have been just a day or two earlier, on February 29th. Mary Jane at once started to work out how many birthdays

I would have had, if this had been the case. Elsbeth wished there was a leap day this year, because then I could ask somebody to marry me. When I reminded her that I was already married to *you* she said that I could ask you again! Would you have liked that? And, what is more, would you have said "Yes"?

Our wedding day – it seems centuries ago. My mother wanted everything to be perfect and in particular she wanted to show your parents *how* perfect it all was. I needed to have lots of bridesmaids, she said. Well, I chose seven, and then she decided that each one was to wear pink silk, but not all the same pink, oh no, the smallest (who was tiny) was to be in the very palest, then up the line, in order of height, each girl was to wear a slightly darker shade. It must have cost the earth, but it did look fantastic.

You told me that I was the most beautiful bride ever. These days when I look at our wedding photo, which always stands on my bedside table, I think that yes, my dress looks lovely, but I look so deadly serious! And I know precisely why: Mother had been so frightfully fussy and worried for months that I tiptoed through the day, scared stiff that anything would go wrong and that she would be furious with me.

My father became very enthusiastic about the wedding as well. His garden was his greatest joy and he had read a lot about the famous landscape gardener Capability Brown, who lived in the 18th century and who created the 'English' garden, moving away from the formal continental style which had been so popular before.

Father told me that Mr Brown, whose real first name was Lancelot, would often say to his patrons that their grounds had huge *capabilities*, hence his nick name. I always thought that Lancelot was not nearly as nice a name, and wondered if his wife called him Capability.

So, our gardeners were busy for months making the place look absolutely wonderful with sloping lawns and steps made of grass and masses of flowers in shades of pink to match the bridesmaids. When one of the gardeners told me that on the great estates, a ha-ha was very much the thing to have, I got really worried. But even father thought that unnecessary: there aren't many sheep in Croydon. We got through the day with my mother actually smiling right until the end, and then a time of absolute bliss began.

Our honeymoon was spent in Austria, where almost immediately you lost your wedding ring on a walk. We searched and searched, but had to give up and then went to a small jeweller's shop and bought a cheap ring, which we were going to replace once we were home. You still have the cheap one on your finger.

We moved into our small flat in Amsterdam where we had those Quaker meetings, and it became one of the happiest times I can remember. To be a Quaker meant a great deal to you. You said that the faith and the nature of a Quaker has two cornerstones: first, the meetings for worship, which have everything to do with loving God, and secondly duty towards society, which has everything to do with love for one's neighbour. "Jesus," you said "called these two loves equal; in other words, loving your neighbour is a way of loving God."

The 'meetings for worship' are for you the very essence of Quakerism. Without a minister, in silence, everyone searches for God's presence. This demands total dedication, and in that silence, now and then, someone will be inspired to say something. I remember how in Woodbrooke our very good elderly friend, David, who taught us young ones about the knowledge and meaning of meetings, once told us the following: "When the urge to speak comes to me, my heart starts to beat faster and at that moment I know that keeping quiet is out of the question."

You always regretted that this deep inspiration came to you only a few times. I don't think it matters at all; your thoughts and your deeds have been, and still are, of much more importance to me and many other people. I was thinking about the expression "keeping quiet" in English. In Dutch there is the one expression for that: "zwijgen", a moving word which really describes the *silence when somebody does not speak*. It is the quality of silence which Jesus created when he refused to answer his accusers, the same silence brave resistance workers create by not answering when they are being interrogated.

In 1935 you changed your job and we had to move to Vaassen, in the middle of the country and far away from Amsterdam and from the Quaker friends we had made; you missed the meetings acutely. Life in general had become difficult: the economic depression which had been debilitating Holland for years and years, deteriorated still further.

In Germany, the National Socialists had become more and more powerful, although at the time we saw it as a purely German problem; we had no idea of the threat that was approaching Europe. We did hear about Germans who had fled their country, who arrived here having left everything behind, telling stories which seemed totally incredible, but we still did not understand what was going on…

My candle is starting to splutter. I'd better blow it out and go upstairs.

Love you,
Isobel

March 1945
Heerenstraat

Darling Jan Willem,

Your younger daughter! Yesterday I had agreed to let Jetje have a meeting with somebody from the Resistance movement in our room; it was to be quite an important discussion, so I had told the girls to stay out of the way. I really thought they had done so, until later that day, when Jetje told me that Elsbeth had walked into the room, looked at the woman who was there with Jetje and asked her, "Are you married?" When the woman replied that no, she was not, Elsbeth said, "Well, I wouldn't bother if I were you," and walked straight out again.

I was *horrified*, but Jetje found it very funny and wondered what you and I had been up to!

Well, later on, when that little episode had gone completely out of my mind, there was a really nasty accident. Elsbeth was playing tag with the other children in the large hall of the house, with its glass panelled doors at one end, and in the midst of the game she skidded on the marble floor, held out an arm to stop herself from falling, and smashed it straight through one of the glass door panels. You wouldn't believe the screams which made all of us come running, and you certainly wouldn't believe the amount of blood streaming from her small, podgy wrist. Katja acted immediately, scooping Elsbeth up in her arms and, after having put lots of cotton cloths round her wrist, running with her – with me behind – to Doctor Hermans, who lives only a few houses away as you know.

Thank God, he was at home and able to deal with things straight away. It was a deep wound, which needed stitching. Elsbeth was very brave throughout it all, and was thrilled to bits when she was told that she would have a large scar on her wrist for the rest of her life.

"It will be your war wound," said Doctor Hermans, and Elsbeth told me that she wanted to show it to lots and lots of people and that she therefore hoped she would live for years and years and years. Let's hope that she will, and may those years be a great deal happier than the ones she is living through now.

This *all* happened yesterday, and now I am sitting at the table, ready to write to you about the small Jewish baby who was whisked away to safety today. As we all know, Jews who are taken away by the Germans are sent to Westerbork, that tiny place in the north east of the country. But that is all we know. What *does* happen to them all?

It was Katja who told me what she'd seen this afternoon. She was standing in a seemingly endless queue for potatoes, when she saw one of

Never again: memorial at Westerbork today

those horrid open wagons being filled up with Jews. Soldiers were standing all around, yelling and shouting, and then suddenly, a young Jewish mother, her baby in her arms, looked desperately around and suddenly darted the few paces to the front of the potato queue and shoved her precious bundle into the arms of a woman. She dashed back to where her husband was standing, knowing that she would be dragged with him onto the waiting wagon. The soldiers had not noticed what had happened; they were far too busy driving and bullying those poor people.

Katja said she would *never* forget the moment when the wagon started to move. At the very back stood the young mother, stumbling a little with the movement of the vehicle and staring at her tiny child, now being held by a stranger. She had sacrificed something she loved more than anything in her world because she was convinced that whatever happened to her baby, it would be spared from the hell she and her husband were entering.

A mother, giving up her child. It is such an *incredible* thing to do and yet it has been done for centuries. The mother of Moses did it – another Jewish mother. The story in the bible never tells us her name, just that she was a woman from the tribe of Levi, living in Egypt, living under the yoke of a tyrant, in exactly the same way as the woman Katja told me about this afternoon. The Pharaoh had ruled that no Jewish boys should be allowed to live; they had to be thrown into the Nile as soon as they were born. Moses' mother, just as the mother of the baby today, refused to let him die. She put him with the utmost care into a cradle made of bulrushes and slid him into the Nile, the same river which had been the grave to so many tiny Jewish boys. A miniature ark, built with the same care as his ancestors' about a thousand years before. That famous story ends with a smile: a kind Egyptian princess found him at the edge of the river and gave him back to his mother, asking her to care for the baby boy until he was grown up and then he would come to live with her in her palace as her son. Of course, we know that this is a miracle story and that this baby boy was spared so that he would be able to save his people and lead them out of Egypt back to the Promised Land. It is unlikely that something as miraculous will happen to the baby saved today, but was what took place today not a kind of miracle? And may, perhaps, *this* baby's story end with a smile?

All my love,
Isobel

March 1945
Heerenstraat

Good news and bad. Elsbeth's wrist is healing well, and although the scar will always be there there is no infection and no pain. However, I am getting worried about your mother; she is looking thin and frail, and no wonder – the food rations by now would be laughable if they were not so serious.

But your mother will never give up, she will carry on fighting for the sake of the country she loves so much. We all know that the home for elderly people she lives in is a beehive of the Resistance. Again and again, people fleeing from the Germans have found a shelter with them. She finds this wonderfully exciting and of course it's precisely what God would want one to do. Oh, I do envy her total, sheer belief in God. She misses your father very much; he really was a wonderful man. I liked him as soon as I met him in the beautiful house in Utrecht your family lived in at the time, when he was General Manager of the Dutch Railways. He was very kind to me, realising more than anybody else in the family that I felt shy and vulnerable. In fact I still have a letter of his, written in his beautiful hand on the rather impressive looking note-paper of the "Hotel Continental" in Paris, dated November 11th 1925. This is what it says:

My dear Isobel,

After a very long meeting of the International Railway Union that made it quite impossible to go to any theatre, I am quite free this evening.

What can I better do than write you at last the letter that I intended to do for months and months? If you would have received all the letters I had the intention to send, you would have a very nice collection (concerning its quantity; I don't talk about its quality because my poor English will always make it very difficult to write to you just as my heart would like to do.)

Today I saw two General Managers of English Railways and not knowing which route you will choose coming to Holland, I have asked them both to look, on the 27th of December, for the nicest little passenger crossing via Folkestone or Harwich, because undoubtedly that passenger will be the daughter in law of their Dutch colleague.

That you will be my daughter in law, my dear, it makes me very happy, not only because I always will be very thankful to those who make my children happy, but I am sure that only a woman's love can complete parents' education.

And my wife and I, we only see the best influence on Jan Willem since he loved you.

I am longing to see you again, it is a long time since we were together in the Queen's Hotel and I am awfully glad you will be staying with us for a few days.

Good bye my dear,
I remain yours most sincerely
Vader

How he would have *hated* to see what is happening to his beloved country, had he lived. As it was, he died in 1935, ten years after he wrote that letter to me. During that time we had been married, and we had Mary Jane and James.

I suddenly remembered the evening when James was just two and your parents were coming to dinner with us; your mother had already arrived, but your father, who had to attend an important meeting, came later. When he walked through the front door, James was sitting on the stairs in his dressing gown. He saw your father and shouted in joyful surprise, "OPA!" At that moment I came into the hall, and I will never forget the look on your father's face. A man who always found it so hard to show his feelings was showing them at that moment: he was enchanted.

He later became Minister of Waterways and in that capacity in 1935 he had to attend the opening of a new bridge, by his beloved Queen Wilhelmina. He was wearing a fantastic dress uniform with a three cornered hat and sword.

It was *very* cold and wet and he was urged to put on an overcoat, but he was not having any of it: he was going to greet his Queen in style. Through no fault of her own, she was very late, and as a result your father caught a severe cold which turned into pneumonia. These were the days before penicillin and a few days later he died. That was the first time I saw you cry.

With all love,
Isobel.

March 1945
Heerenstraat

The second and last time I saw you cry was at the very beginning of the war, on May 10th 1940. At dawn it promised to be a glorious spring day, one of those without a cloud in the sky, but then we heard it, a soft, distant humming that drew nearer and nearer. It grew louder, first a sinister droning and then suddenly a deafening, roaring sound above our heads and we could see them, the German planes on their way to invade our country. You stood there at the window with tears streaming down your face; they weren't just tears of sadness, these were tears of furious anger and indignation:

"How *dare* they come into our country and take away our freedom!"

It was this same feeling of anger and indignation that gave rise to the Resistance Movement, with so many people finding the courage during the following five years to help those in danger, and it is still this same feeling which gives all of us the power to be brave, stand up to the wrong that is being done to us and battle through – all this, of course, without letting the children know how frightening it all is.

I am perfectly sure that that same anger and indignation would have engulfed the British people if they had been invaded by the Germans and they would have reacted with the same courage as the Dutch have shown. Thank God they weren't, and thank God they are fighting for us.

That sunny day in May was the first of five days of ferocious fighting: in the north near the big dam across the north of the IJsselmeer, the lake which was previously known as the Zuider Zee; in the west where German sea planes landed on the river Maas and where so many bridges had to be defended; in the east on the Grebbe-Line, towards the German border.

The German soldiers, many of whom were young boys, must have been thunderstruck by this Dutch rebellion, having been totally convinced that we would receive them with open arms because that is what their leaders had told them. They had been led to believe they were going to liberate and enrich us, so I can well imagine their utter frustration, which grew into anger as the war years went on. Their officers were not only frustrated by the Dutch reaction, they were *furious*.

On May 14th, when the Dutch had still not given up the fight, the Dutch officer in command of Rotterdam was ordered to end any further resistance. He was warned that if not, the town would be bombed and, if necessary, the bombing of Amsterdam, The Hague, Utrecht and Haarlem would follow. At 1.30 that same afternoon it happened: the centre of Rotterdam was destroyed within a quarter of an hour. Quarter of an hour! To the inhabitants it must have felt an eternity. Thus, after five days of fierce resistance it was all over and the occupation of Holland had begun.

Bombing of Rotterdam, May 1940

Do you remember how frantic we were about James? We heard on the news what was happening to Rotterdam and I could see in my mind the waves of huge flames reaching out everywhere, enveloping the houses, the streets and the people. James was there, but neither you nor I could do anything to protect our son from harm.

Then came the call from Sis to say that all was well; the bombardment had not reached the outskirts where she lived. The relief inside me was immense, followed immediately by a deep feeling of guilt: I should not feel happy for my son when so many others had perished in this hell of fire and ash.

In a way it seems as if it was just yesterday, that afternoon when the heart was ripped out of Rotterdam. At other times it feels like centuries ago, centuries of hunger and cold and darkness and fear.

All my love
Isobel

March 1945
Heerenstraat

You know Darling, I do wish I could write to my parents and tell
them what it is really like to be occupied, describing everyday life with a
foreign ruler in your country. Of course, they will have read about brave
soldiers fighting on the battlefield, about brave aircrew fighting in the sky
and brave sailors in terrible danger on the seas.

I will *never* underestimate what those men are going through.
Evening after evening, listening secretly to our radios, we admire them,
applaud them, and are deeply grateful for what they are doing for us. I
know that my parents, too, will be full of gratitude for those soldiers and
will be reading every article, following them every step of the way. But
what is happening to the ordinary people here is something they have not
the slightest idea of; they will be able to understand at least something
of what the soldiers are going through, but I don't think we in occupied
Holland are understood at all.

The first thing that happened, once we were occupied, was that we
had to bring everything of value to our town hall. We were told to hand
in jewellery, fur coats, radios, pictures and many more items. Immediately
the Dutch hid as many things as they could, creating ingenious hiding
places. Fantastic stories went around about the way in which people kept
beloved belongings away from our new rulers: rings and other small items
of jewellery were put in the bottom of the flour tin, the flour gently laid
over them like a blanket; silk rugs were hidden under ordinary carpets;
paintings, carefully wrapped, went into the cellars to live under the
potatoes; the medicine cupboard in bathrooms and empty pillowcases in
the linen cupboard were also used. When we reported to the town hall on
that beautiful spring day I was almost melting wearing the favourite fur
jacket your sister had bought me some years before. I was not going to give
that up, so I put it on under my winter coat. I must have looked absurd:
the weather was glorious that May and there I was, walking about like an

overfilled stocking. Nobody noticed. There were far more serious things to think about.

I often wondered in those first days why the weather kept on being so wonderful; why was there not a continual downpour of rain to reflect the sorrow of a country that was crying tears of anguish and anger and fear?

I still have that special jacket hanging well behind our everyday clothes, and sometimes I go upstairs and touch the soft fur and feel quite triumphant that it is still there and what fun it was to hide it the way I did that day.

Even more entertaining was the story about Karel van Voort and his car. He was a very close friend of ours, a farmer living on his beloved farm out in the country, not so very far away from Apeldoorn, the town where we live. From the moment the Germans set foot over the border into our country, Karel had been absolutely *livid*; he certainly wasn't going to give them anything that he owned, and of all the things he *did* possess, his car was the most precious of all.

Furiously and without ever pausing for breath, he dug an enormous hole in his farmyard and, with the help of his sons, lowered the car into it. I am sure this lodging under the ground is not doing the car much good, but at least nobody will lay his hands on it. He was our rock right from the start, managing to get food to our house again and again throughout the first three years, and when the Germans started to raid his farm and fields, he gave us the addresses of friends of his who had farms deeper in the country.

He and his sons came over on that fateful evening in 1943 when we heard that our house was going to be taken by Germans, doing everything they could to help us remove our most precious belongings from the house. Karel stayed the night, much to the delight of the girls, who adore him. For me it was the one thing I needed in the turmoil of what was happening to us along with the bewilderment at your arrest and imprisonment in Vught.

He still comes to visit us now and then and those days are highlights;

he never arrives empty-handed and brings us wonderful gifts such as fresh eggs or a piece of liver sausage. I only wish you could share some of those things with us. Our rations are now slight, but we are still managing to have enough food to get through the days, but you tell me that in your tiny, crowded house food is becoming desperately scarce. Even the once wealthy Jewish couple in the house have hardly anything left of their capital. A few slices of rye bread are sometimes all you have in a day and you try and make them last as long as you can, allowing yourself a tiny bite every few hours. God, when all this is over, how we will enjoy every single morsel of food! Wonderful to 'talk' to you like this most evenings and although you can't hear me, I know you are listening.

Isobel

March 1945
Heerenstraat

Darling,

I have just read again a letter sent to you by your brother Hans, another reminder of those very first days of the war. It was dated May 17th, exactly one week after the occupation, and this is what he wrote:

Dear Jan Willem,

Mother was here today and not only did she tell me that you are all safe and well, something I am very happy about, but she also told me about you going to the Hembrug in Amsterdam to join the factory workers in their strike against the Occupier. The factory produces guns and other

artillery equipment and of course this is all going to be taken to Germany. Those brave guys went on strike for one day and many people went to join and support them. And one of them was you.

I can tell you that I thanked God when I heard what you had done. It was such a wonderful contrast to the tales of betrayal I had been told about.

It did me a lot of good, and has made me feel very grateful. I am so proud my own brother behaved so courageously. You know very well that we have not always got on very well and that I often thought of you as a strange chap, but after this, I will never blame you for anything, ever.

I know that the Dutch surrender was necessary, but at the going down of the sun over our fatherland I cried, something I had not done since Father's death. Yet I believe in the great strength of our nation and I hope and sincerely believe that our children will grow up free and independent citizens of the Netherlands.

Mother is well and very happy to know that she will be going to the home for elderly ladies in Apeldoorn. We went to have a look at it and her room looks wonderful with a nice view of the garden. The staff seem very kind and it will be good to know that you and the family are in the same town and so near. Mother told me that she is especially looking forward to visits from Elsbeth. There seems to be a very close friendship there!

My very best wishes to you, to Isobel and the children from, believe me, your dearest brother and friend,
Hans

What a wonderful letter for you to receive from Hans, who was always looking down on you and who always thought he was so much better than you at everything. In this short letter he has admitted that he was wrong and he sees you now with the love and respect you so deserve.

You never told me about this trip to Amsterdam. Well, you said you were going to see some people there, but I had no idea that you were going in order to demonstrate your feelings against the enemy. Mind you, I'm not surprised you didn't tell me; I would have been worried stiff and I would have tried to stop you. I bet Mary Jane and Elsbeth would have *loved* to know…. gosh, they would have been proud of you.

And those stories of betrayal Hans mentioned? So many rumours were flying about in those early days of the war. One was that collaborators gave Dutch uniforms to the Germans soldiers who were fighting their way into the islands south of Rotterdam, to make the going very much easier; it is simply unbelievable.

Another game they played was spreading defeatist rumours; it's incredible how people take in such stories and immediately believe them. It all helped to pave the way for the occupier. And then there were the stories spread by the occupier. We were told that the invasion had nothing to do with hostility or enmity and that, on the contrary, it was the English and French who had planned to invade Holland and rule over it. Documents were going to be produced to prove this fact. The Germans had come to their rescue. Never would they allow a Germanic sister nation like Holland to fall into foreign hands. They had come to protect us.

Many people believed them. Many people *wanted* to believe them. It was going to be all right. After all, schools, churches, police stations and council offices were left to continue as normal. The fact that the Swastika was raised above all official buildings was something one should not worry about too much…

It worried you a great deal. You were so right. By the end of May, that month full of sunshine and full of overpowering sadness, the Germans took over the civil administration, its leader being Seyss Inquart, who, like his Führer, was Austrian by birth. His German officials poured in and drop by drop, ever so slowly, the new regime took over. You detested the appearance of the Swastika, flown on virtually every building. To see it there in place of our own red, white and blue flag was perhaps the most poignant way in which to tell the Dutch that their country had been taken over.

And your indignation at the stupidity of their choice! The swastika is an ancient symbol, revered by Buddhists, Hindus, Celts and North American Indians. Peoples and tribes who used this symbol, believed to signify prosperity and creativity, would have looked up to the swastika with deep respect. And then the Nazis adopted it, convinced that is was a symbol of pure "Aryan" origin.

Another notion which made you so furious was that Hitler told his followers that the German nation was the purest example of the Aryan race and thereby the supreme bearers of culture.

There is still now a rumour going round that some of these pure Aryans were busy working out a system of local government for Great Britain, writing down exactly who was going to be burgomaster of which town or village.

HOW DARE THEY!

Your very indignant, but very loving
Isobel

P.S. A story I heard to cheer you up: A member of the Resistance was warned by a neighbour that his house was surrounded by Germans and that a raid was imminent. While the Germans were searching the house, they noticed a light on in the WC. One of the soldiers rattled the handle of the locked door and ordered the person in there to come out. "Yes, yes," answered a woman's voice, "I am coming." There was the sound of flushing and then a servant girl came out, mumbling "Enschuldigung" (I am sorry) to the soldier. When the Germans had left, the owner of the house came out of the WC... Brilliant!

March 1945
Heerenstraat

My dearest Jan Willem,

Today is James's birthday. It is hard to believe that he is 13 years old now. It is also a miracle that Sis Mulder is still so happy to keep him under her wing. It is not easy for her. You and I had decided to let James go to a primary school in Rotterdam, but it did not work out at all: he was teased again and again, it made him angry and violent clashes occurred. So Sis decided to teach him herself right through those school years. She is doing wonders, especially in Maths and Music.

Reading is still a problem; he isn't interested in imaginary stories; he isn't interested in the shaping of a sentence; all he wants to know about is his maths and his music (very close friends!). But she won't be able to work these miracles for ever. Soon his age will be beyond her teaching capabilities, made worse by the fact that his epileptic attacks are becoming more frequent and more serious. We can't expect her to cope with all this, but what are we to do?

She has told me that she is determined to have him in her home. She isn't going to give him up to anybody – not even his parents. She knows jolly well that you are working in the Resistance Movement and that I am living in two very small rooms with the girls in a house which is not even our own. Katja and Maurits are giving up so much for us already; we could never ask them to have James, with all his problems, in their home as well.

So, thank God for Sis. She told me that James was playing a short piece by Mozart, and a visitor to the house, who was a musician himself, asked James to play the same piece in the way Haydn would have composed it. He did. Then he asked him to do the same in the way Beethoven would have composed it. James did.

Darling, we obviously have a very gifted child, but how he will be able to use that gift in his future life, I have absolutely no idea.

I talked about it with Mary Jane this afternoon. I think she finds it quite hard to say what she really feels about James. Of course, she was the only one for nearly all of her first three years, adored by everyone, clever, pretty, full of fun, totally bilingual and having our attention all day long. And then James arrived, and with him all the worries and sadness and the need for so much care. She had been told by lots of grown ups how lovely it was going to be to have a brother or sister to play with and now, instead of an amusing little boy or girl, here was a tiny baby which cried a lot, was very often terribly unwell and with whom Mary Jane was expected to be gentle and understanding – not easy for a robust toddler.

When James, at long last, started to crawl and became more interesting for her, she started to be a real little mother to him, but it didn't last very long; his slowness irritated her and his epileptic fits and hefty tantrums frightened her. And, something she would never admit to us and perhaps not even to herself, is that she has never been able to accept him as he is.

For Elsbeth it has been so much easier, because he was her big brother from when she was born and although she could see that he was a bit different from other children's big brothers, that did not bother her at

Mary Jane in 1941
aged 12

all. By the time she grew a little bit older, James had gone to Sis Mulder in Rotterdam. Darling, it is getting late. There is something I find very worrying and frightening, but I am so tired and cold, it is better that I tell you tomorrow.

Miss you so very much,
Isobel

March 1945
Heerenstraat

A few days ago, Mary Jane and Hannie, her closest friend, told me
that they had spent some time with a few school pals, singing anti-German
songs. The Dutch love doing it: they think of a very well known Dutch song
and then put new words to it, describing the occupiers or the collaborators.
They showed me the words of one song that describes a collaborator trying
to sell the NSB paper, the rag published by the National Socialist Bond or
Dutch Nazi organisation, which they have the cheek to call 'Fatherland'.
I remember how furious you were when you heard that title for the first
time. Well, this is one of the songs being produced and I think it rather
good.

On the side of the street
Stands a freedom hater.
Not a he, not a she:
A collaborator!
With his rag in his hand
He is very willing
To sell his own 'Fatherland'
For less than a shilling.

It sounded fantastic in Dutch and I thought it would be fun to make
an English translation. You're the linguist, I am sure you would have made
a better job of it, but I was quite pleased with mine. Mary Jane and Hannie
told me that they had seen such a collaborator, selling that awful paper, the
other day and they recognised him; he had been a pupil in their school.
Worse still, they went on to say that they had seen Karin with him several
times. I know you always find it hard to remember people's names, but
you must still remember Michiel and Anke, who live just outside Apeldoorn
– well, Karin is their daughter. We used to see quite a lot of each other

before the war and I was very fond of her especially. Jan Willem, what was I going to do? Here was a friend of our family being seen in the company of someone trying to sell that filth!

My first impulse was to talk to Anke at once, but then I thought it over and I decided to speak to Karin myself. She is a lovely girl, we get on very well and I hoped she would tell me what is really going on. She came today. Mary Jane had concocted some story of having problems with a chemistry question (the few remaining teachers are very good at distributing home-work for their pupils, thereby trying to keep our children at least a little bit up to date with their school subjects) and she lured Karin here with the promise of some potato cake I had managed to make with some very original ingredients…

After the chemistry homework which did not take long at all (no wonder, it's so cold in that bedroom), the girls came down. Mary Jane left after muttering a rather lame excuse and Karin immediately realised what was going on. She didn't mind; in fact I think she was very relieved to talk about this huge thing she could not even begin to mention to her parents. It appears that she had started to "fall in love" with Pieter about a year ago; it must be admitted that he's a very attractive, tall, good-looking boy with the most amazing blue eyes. I'm sure she's not the only girl who believes that she's 'fallen in love' with him – in the way that fourteen to fifteen year olds do.

In whatever way these two felt about each other, they certainly appear to have been able to open their hearts and talk about their innermost feelings. This must have been a revelation for Pieter because talking about your feelings was not something done in his family. His father was the problem; equally handsome and tall and with those same piercing blue eyes, he always expected more from Pieter than he could give. However much he tried, it was never good enough: when he came home with a 9/10 for an essay his father would want to know why he didn't get 10. If Pieter scored the winning goal at a school hockey match, he would grumble that the previous goal was scored by someone else and not by his son.

"And his mother?" I asked.

Poor woman, she is the gentle kind who lets everybody run roughshod over her, while her husband – jovial and thoughtful to his friends – is actually a domineering ogre to his wife and child at home.

The major problem is the fact that Pieter's mother is not only gentle, but she is actually very unwell. Karin does not know what is wrong exactly and Pieter is apparently rather vague about it, but I do know myself that she always looks pale and tired and needs to rest a lot. Pieter told Karin that his father always becomes very irritated with his wife's illnesses; he wants her around as little as possible and sends her to bed whenever he feels she is being a nuisance. This has been going on for years. Even as a small boy Pieter used to have breakfast by himself, his father having left for work and his mother upstairs in bed. Just before leaving for school he would go and say goodbye to her, a moment they both enjoyed. But the best part of the day was when he came home in the afternoon and they could be together without any intrusion from anyone. During the week he never went to other boys' houses and no friend was invited to his. At the weekend, when his father ruled, it was trips to the hockey club, outings with boys from his class to the cinema, swimming pool or picnics in the woods, all organised by his father, while his mother was left at home, alone.

No wonder that this boy not only began to hate his father as he grew older, but he also became convinced that the only person in the world who loved him was his powerless mother. He became a very shy and introvert teenager, polite, hard-working at his schoolwork, liked by the other pupils, but only from a distance; Pieter would never let anyone come really near him. This was exactly the kind of youngster the N.S.B. or Dutch National Socialist Union was looking for. These collaborators were always on the lookout for more recruits and would approach vulnerable young men like Pieter, telling them how much they were needed and how much good they would be doing for their country. They would persuade them to join them by saying how well Germany was doing, how Adolf Hitler had brought back order, employment, discipline and wealth and how the same would

106

be the reward for the Dutch if only the Führer was believed and followed here.

"He believed them," said Karin, "he's totally convinced they are right and he's proud to stand on the corner of the street with that awful paper called *Fatherland*, because he is convinced that what he's doing is precisely for the good of his own country, his fatherland. He doesn't realise what they are doing to him and, which is more frightening, he feels he is wanted and appreciated, something that has never happened to him before.

"And the terrible thing," she continued, "is that I love him. I hate what he is doing and I tell him that over and over again, and yet I love him. We have the most outrageous arguments – I have even *hit* him – but it's no use. He believes he is right even though I *know* he is wrong, but still I love him." I really admire this young girl. Dear heaven, what our children have to live through!

Dutch collaborators were arrested and tried
after the end of the war.

After careful thought (and wishing that you, who are so good at this sort of thing, could be beside me...) I said to her that if Pieter is so sure that he's right, he should accept the fact that people who think the opposite are equally right in their own minds. I advised her to point out to him that it is becoming glaringly clear that what the Germans promised us during the invasion is not quite coming true (to put it very mildly!). I also suggested that she may still love him, but that she should make it clear that if even *one* Dutch person is killed through his involvement with the N.S.B. she will leave him forever.

We talked for quite a long time. I feel so much for this young girl who really should be having lots of fun with all her friends, being able to go out at night, going to dances and walking home in the dark, feeling totally safe and coming home to windows lit by lamps rather than the awful blackout curtains which cover not just light, but also any welcoming warmth. I pray that she will be able to convince Pieter. The big problem of course is that it will be nigh impossible for him to leave that awful Party now, even if he wants to. The only solution will be the end of this awful war. Wild rumours are flying about everywhere: the Germans are losing on every front, and are becoming desperate. They now take anything they want or need, ignoring international regulations as if they had never even existed: food of any kind, farmers' carts, bicycles, and believe it or not I even heard about an ambulance being taken; the ambulance was stopped, the wounded were lifted out and laid down on the side of the road and the vehicle driven away by German soldiers to be used for whatever purpose they chose. You think you have heard the worst story, but then something even more awful is being whispered about. Thank God for the courageous Dutch who secretly write songs like the one I've quoted. Let's hope that before long we'll be able to sing our 'forbidden songs' at the top of our voices.

Love you so very much.
Isobel

March 1945
Heerenstraat

Hello Darling,

Katja is just wonderful. She's taken us into her home, providing miraculous meals; she's a great friend for Mary Jane and a wonderful 'aunt' for Elsbeth, and she helps everybody she meets. Here's another example:

Just before seven o'clock one evening the front door bell rang; I went out to answer the door, but Katja was there before me. On the doorstep stood a bedraggled, very thin woman, who said in a soft voice, "Hello Katja, do you remember me?" She went on to explain that they had been at school together and had kept in touch for some years, really just a card now and then. Apparently she lives in Amsterdam and had walked into the countryside hoping to find some food at a farm somewhere, but now it was too late and she would have to try the following day. She'd heard that Katja still lived here and well, here she was …

I was sure that Katja hardly remembered her at all, but that would not stop her from inviting this woman, who was almost dying on her feet from starvation, into her living room. She stayed with us for a week, and was able to tell us what was happening in the west of the country. By the end of January the ration per week for each member of the population in the western cities was: one small clammy loaf of bread, ½oz of butter, ½oz of meat of very inferior quality, 2lbs of potatoes, 2ozs of vermicelli and ½oz of cheese. That was it, and then only if it was available in the shops after a long queueing session.

When I told Elsbeth about this, she did not think that their rations were too bad. "Darling," I said, "that means that everybody in the west can only eat one slice of that awful bread, a tiny bit of butter, a miniscule piece of meat, a small part of a potato, one slice of cheese and a very small bit of vermicelli during the whole of a day." "Gosh, yes," she said, "we are still lucky compared to that."

Compared to that... I am so pleased that she realised, but I did not tell her the next bit of Katja's school friend's story – that thousands of men and women with wheelbarrows, prams or any other kind of vehicle are walking from the west to parts of the country where there is even a tiny hope of food to be had. In this incredibly harsh winter many of these famished people don't reach the place they are aiming for. Sadly, in the few clothes they have, and wearing only threadbare gym shoes or even no footwear at all, the icy cold or the malnutrition kills them. Then it's the awful duty of the relatives to carry back their corpses. Compared to that... my younger daughter is so right.

Wish you were here to talk to her. (And to me....)
Isobel

March 1945
Heerenstraat

My Darling,

We are now nearing the end of March. In a month and a bit it will be 10th May again, the anniversary of the invasion. I was thinking back again to those first few days and the way we hid anything precious to us.

Most precious of all was our Queen and her family and it was imperative that they were 'hidden' at once. We will always remember how reluctant Queen Wilhelmina was to leave her people: it was said that if it had been up to her, she would have gone to the Grebbe Line towards the Eastern border of the country with a gun in her hand...

She knew very well that this was not possible and she immediately organised for her daughter Crown Princess Juliana and the Princess's two tiny daughters to be taken to England and to safety. Later they would travel on to Canada. She herself arrived in England on the 13th, determined to fight for her country in whatever way she could.

You have always been fiercely proud of the Dutch royal family, a monarchy nowhere near as old as the one which has ruled in my country since the 11th century – there was no "Kingdom of Oranje Nassau" until 1815. Nassau was a small German duchy, where Count William lived quietly until in 1544 the Netherland branch of the family died out and the 11-year-old William inherited the principality of Orange, in the south of France. He had become the Prince of Oranje Nassau.

There were, however, conditions to the inheritance. The Emperor, Charles V, expected him to come and live in The Netherlands to be trained in the ways of an important nobleman. He had to learn French and the history and language of his new country. He was to become the famous William the Silent, who led the revolt of The Netherlands against the occupation of Spain. He would have been proud of his descendant Wilhelmina, who is now defending The Netherlands against another occupier.

Thank God we still have her as our Queen. When her father, King William III, died, his daughter (and only child) was just ten and so became a very young Queen indeed. Her mother, Queen Emma, acted as her regent until Wilhelmina was eighteen. When she had been on the throne for forty-eight years, she considered the idea of abdicating in favour of her daughter Juliana; (Juliana was named after the mother of William the Silent). The Government thought differently and persuaded her to continue. By then it was 1938…

I always find it such a coincidence that it looks as if you have to be born on the last day of the month if you want to inherit the Dutch throne… Wilhelmina was born on the 31st August, Juliana on the 30th April and Beatrix, her oldest daughter on January 31st. She will be our Queen one day, unless a baby brother comes along. If so, he'd better be born at the very end of a month.

I'm tired after all that history. You often used to talk about all this, and I know how much it means to you – it was good to put it down on paper, and good to concentrate on something other than how much food I'll be able to scrape together for the next few meals.

All my love
Isobel

The last day of March 1945
Heerenstraat

Karel van der Voort came for a visit, and what a day it has been! Mary Jane asked him straight away if he had been able to have a peek at his car which is still lying there under the ground in his farm yard. He told her that he wanted to keep it a surprise for liberation day.

"And that," he said, "is not far off." I wish I could believe him. The stories around us are so depressing; more and more people are being arrested; again and again you hear about totally innocent men and sometimes women being shot…

When I said that to him he took my hands in his and with that understanding smile he said:

"All that is true and it is terrifying and heartbreaking, but it is because our enemy is desperate. He knows he is losing this war; no, I am sure he knows he has *already* lost it. So now he does everything in his power to hurt and destroy what is no longer his. Isobel, and you too, Mary Jane and your little sister, you have been very brave for a long time: hold on, don't give in. I promise you, we are nearly there." We all hugged each other and then the girls went out to hunt for some kindling.

"I have brought you a small present." Karel took out of his pocket a parcel wrapped in newspaper. I noticed when I started to take away the paper that it was German, 'yelling' in huge letters that the Führer was winning, that he would protect the Dutch from British tyranny…

What was inside was quite the opposite. Strange, how I had been thinking and writing about the Queen last night, because there in my hand was a tiny silver spoon. The bowl was a silver 'kwartje' or a 25 cent coin; at the top of the handle was a 'dubbeltje' or ten cent one, both engraved with the Queen's head.

I had heard that items were being made from the coins we used in our country before the war. Most of those coins had been taken by the Germans, but quite a few were hidden during the invasion and later shaped into wonderful treasures like the one I now held up to the light of the afternoon sun streaming through the window. I was so excited that I said without thinking:

"What a wonderful thing to write about tonight!"

"What do you mean Isobel, 'write about?' What do you write and to whom?"

I had to tell him how during many late evenings, sometimes well into the night, I write down the things that have been happening and my feelings about them.

"In English," I added lamely.

Karel, who had been standing next to me at the window, lowered himself slowly into a chair and just stared at me.

"I don't send them to anyone; I just hide each piece of paper I have written on before I go to bed," I said.

"Right," sighed Karel. "First of all, I want to see your hiding place. Next, there should not be just one hiding place, you must spread your risk.

I suppose the girls know what you are doing, do they?" I nodded, but told him that they would never say a word about it to anyone. That I had made them swear.

He believed me. He knows as well as I do how much the children are involved with the dangers in our occupied country.

"And you are absolutely sure that nobody else has an inkling of what you are doing, not even the very people you share this house with?"

"Not a soul," I told him.

We then covered a few sheets at a time with newspaper and Karel found the most incredible hiding places to put them in. Not even Mary Jane and Elsbeth are going to be told about them, he made me promise that. He really is a genius, but then, I know he, too, has had to hide quite a few secrets during the last few years.

"Do you have enough paper and ink?" he asked, "I noticed that the last few pages were written in pencil."

"I have enough sheets of paper; I tear them out of the girls' exercise books, they have got lots of them," I said. "I have very small handwriting, so I don't need much paper, but yes, I have run out of ink. Writing with a pencil is not easy and it's difficult to see what you are doing by the light of one candle."

Bless him, he promised me that he would come again in a few days' time and bring ink with him. I did not ask him how he would get hold of something like that – one just doesn't.

So now, Darling, I finish this letter, written with my pencil and am very much looking forward to being able to use the fountain pen again, which you gave me all those years ago.

I love you, but I love Karel *almost* as much.
Isobel

April 1945
Heerenstraat

Darling,

The first of April has gone by without any silly jokes, or so I thought.

Mary Jane told me that she and some of her friends directed a German soldier, who asked them the way to somewhere, in exactly the opposite direction, all standing there very erect, very polite, and smiling…

You would have loved that.

We crept up into the loft again last night and listened to Queen Wilhelmina. It is so moving to hear her warm, heartfelt voice telling us to hold on, to have courage, that she lives with us at every moment. She always ends by saying:

"Countrymen, we are one more day nearer peace."

Karel came again today with enough ink to write a novel! It was lovely that he came so soon and it is a delight to use my pen again. He even brought a few more candles. I wonder if he got them from some church, they are so fat.

He said something really wonderful to me. I had been feeling a bit guilty – scared even – because he had clearly been so worried about me writing to you in the way I do. He told me that he had thought about it and decided that I was doing absolutely the right thing.

"You see," he said, "after the war, after all this is over and everybody tries to build up a life again, let alone build up the country from the ruins it is in now, I think very, very few people will want to, or even feel able to, talk about what has been happening to them over the last five years. The letters you write are therefore important. Just keep going."

I said something about us listening to the Queen last night and then he told me what a fantastic rock she is, over there in London.

I had had no idea, but in that city she has opened a house for those brave Dutch men (and even women, Karel told me) who cross the North Sea in whatever way they can to reach England and then join the Allied Forces to help bring victory to all the occupied lands.

Dear God, these people are brave. When you think how often those journeys can go wrong. Just imagine the wind blowing from the wrong direction, and those (very often) tiny ships floating helplessly straight into the arms of the German Warships.

Queen Wilhelmina, so Karel told me, offers this house in London to those Dutch people who have sailed to England, to have a chance to meet, take a rest, share a drink, talk to each other and relax. The house is called 'Oranjehaven' or in English, 'Orange Harbour'.

The Queen has said to the men, who are often very young:

"You are the link between me and those who had to stay at home."

She insists on meeting every one of them and, over a cup of tea, she prompts them to tell her all that is happening in her country in the greatest detail.

What a fabulous thing to know that this is happening in England. That there are so many people thinking about us and who are determined to come and help.

My pen just keeps going tonight, not only because it is so much easier to write with than the stubs of pencils I have been using lately, but also because I can't help looking back and wanting to get everything down in writing. It's getting late, but there is just one more story before I go upstairs.

In January 1943 Princess Juliana was in Canada with her two tiny daughters, Beatrix and Irene. She was also expecting another baby, due to be born any day. If this baby was a boy, under Dutch law he would be the successor to the throne, *but* – he would have to be born on Dutch soil.

A problem! Well, the Canadians solved it by donating the ward on which this baby was going to be born to the Dutch nation. This must surely have become the smallest colony in the world ...

However, after all that, it was yet another girl: on January 19th Princess

Margriet was born. What a day for everybody in this country: a brand new Princess of Orange, far away from Holland, but also far away from any danger. And as close to the Dutch people as it was possible to be.

I was thinking about the names of those three princesses out there in Canada and what their names signify.

Beatrix means "Blessed voyager through life". Well, she the oldest, just six months younger than Elsbeth, certainly has travelled a long way already in her short life. Pray God that she will soon be on her journey back to Holland.

Irene means "Peace." One could not think of a better name for a princess who had to flee her country as a 9-month-old baby. May the meaning of her name soon be welcomed and embraced by millions of people all over Europe.

Margriet means "Pearl", something pure and protected in its shell. This tiny baby is just that. And of course hers is also the name of the pearly white daisy that's flowering in the meadows, however occupied we might be.

I wonder if Princess Juliana has realised that she is now the "Mother of Pearl."

Yes, it is high time for bed. Sleep well darling,
Isobel

April 1945
Heerenstraat

Good morning, Darling

Although it was very late last night before I finally went to bed, I woke up well before anybody else in the house and went for a walk in the garden. A heavy dew was sparkling on the cobwebs and the early sunshine was bathing them in colours of the rainbow. The last of the snowdrops are still there in the sheltered places and it made me think of Princess Margriet and the white flower she symbolises.

A white flower, like her father's – but in his case it is a white *carnation*. He always wears one in his lapel and right from the beginning of the war, every year on his birthday, the 29th June, many people have worn a white carnation. Oh, the N.S.B. lot don't like that *at all*; eventually they started to tear them from people's coats. And that, they thought, was that.

Well, it wasn't. The next year, people were wearing the forbidden flower again, this time with a darning needle firmly fixed behind it … the Dutch certainly know how to say it with flowers. When, at the very beginning of the war, the Germans strictly forbade any mention of members of the Royal Family, on August 2nd that year the statues of Queen Emma, Wilhelmina's beloved mother, both in The Hague and in Amsterdam, were covered in flowers: it was her birthday.

Jetje is a star. You see, I really want to go and see James again, but I don't think I can make the journey any longer. Mary Jane has totally forbidden me to even try. She says I am looking so thin and tired and worn out that she simply won't *let* me go. Bless her, she even offered to go herself, but then it was my turn to become bossy. Can you imagine it, a rather pretty looking girl like our daughter on an old bike, all the way to Rotterdam!

And then Jetje arrived. She wanted to know how we all were and if there was any news about you. I think she was quite shocked to see me having gone down hill so much. She immediately suggested that she should go and visit James herself. James knows and adores her – all children do. She would be there and back in a few days, she said, and tell me all about him.

"Give me some of that awful chicory stuff we call coffee," she said, "and let's try and talk about what is *really* bothering you, because it is quite clear that something is."

She was, as always, quite right. The story about Karin and Pieter was something I could not discuss with anybody in the house or among near friends and neighbours, but I could with Jetje. After I'd told the story, I asked her if I ought to talk about all this with Pieter's parents.

"Absolutely not," answered Jetje. "First of all, Karin has spoken to you in strictest confidence. Secondly, it is not as if Pieter's parents are friends of yours and how do you know in what way they would react? You told me that *he* is difficult and does not like his son and *she* is weak, almost an invalid, and would be totally unable to cope with you coming along with your story. They might not even be aware of what Pieter is doing."

"But what do you think he *is* doing, working with the N.S.B.?" I wondered. "How can he support those collaborators, who right from the start with their 'National Socialist Ideals' have tried to undermine their fellow countrymen and done so much damage to the Resistance?"

"I don't know," she replied. "I'm glad to say I never belonged to that lot, but I wouldn't think Pieter is doing much more than sticking up posters (and tearing down the ones the Resistance bravely put up during the night), selling that ghastly newspaper of theirs and things like that.

Far more serious is what these people are doing to his mind, possibly getting him ready for "greater things"; but let's hope that all the rumours we hear are correct, that the end of all this really is near and there won't be any more opportunities for Pieter to learn or do any more."

The girls came back at that moment with quite a lot of tiny bits of wood they had gathered. Even those twigs will give a bit of warmth for a little while. Great!

Jetje played a few games of Ludo with them. The Dutch give that game the title "Man, don't get annoyed!" Most appropriate for Mary Jane, who hates losing.

Jetje left well before dark with little presents for Sis and James and a few pieces of food we had been able to scramble together. Elsbeth had drawn a card for her brother with all of us on it. You were in the picture drawn by your daughter as well, looking very fat and healthy. I know it is not quite like that in reality. Look after yourself, Darling, as much as you can. We all love you and need you.

Isobel

April 1945
Heerenstraat

Darling Jan Willem

Last night in bed I was thinking about what I said at the end of my letter and it made me remember when, not long before the war, we went to a concert. It was just about the time when I had realised that I had to say things twice, sometimes three times, to you before you answered.

Having grown up with deaf parents, I recognised the signs and started to wonder if your hearing was all it should be; your own grandfather started to become deaf in his early forties, so there was even more reason to go into the matter.

We went to an ear specialist who was wonderful, extremely thorough when examining you and very kind and understanding when he told you that you had indeed just, and only just, started to lose some of your hearing. And then, very gently, almost apologetically, he told you that it was likely that you would become extremely, if not totally, deaf in your later years.

I remember sitting there in the corner of the room and feeling so dreadfully sorry for you. And I started to have feelings of foreboding: a future with a repetition of my childhood, teenage and young adult years, demanding unrelenting patience and understanding on my part. Of course, you showed no sign of what was going on inside you. That has always been your way and it was no surprise to me, but I think the specialist was a bit puzzled.

Then he asked if you had had any experience of tinnitus, a continuous ringing sound in the ear. You had not, but it was an interesting question, because your grandfather suffered from tinnitus a great deal before his deafness started to develop in earnest.

Not long after that consultation we went to a concert in the Small Chamber of the Concertgebouw in Amsterdam. The first string quartet by Smetana, the Czech composer, was being played: music which describes his life, and most importantly, his oncoming deafness. In the fourth movement there's a sudden, long and piercing high-pitched note depicting the tinnitus which, as Smetana wrote, "announced the start of my troubles." By the time he was fifty he had become totally deaf and he died ten years later, insane, in an asylum.

At the end of the concert we went home spellbound by the beauty of the music and by the story it had told us. Much later, unable to get to sleep, I lay wondering if genius always has to go hand in hand with sadness or disability. I so very much hope that your hearing is still good enough to keep you out of danger, that you are able to pick up any warning signs. I know you would not dream of giving up what you are doing, but please take care, for your sake, for our sake and for the sake of all those who work with you.

We love and miss you so very much,
Isobel

April 1945
Heerenstraat

My dear Jan Willem,

Matches: we are running out! They are becoming really difficult to get hold of and they are *vital*, both for trying to light the stove in order to burn the bits of wood we still have left and for lighting my candle by which to write at night. We now carefully cut the remaining few matches in two or even three, and light each tiny bit as we need it from the dying fire or the stub of a candle.

But when I heard the stories from Jetje about the tragedy in the west of the country, I realised that here we are still relatively lucky. It'll be easy to forget this though, when I'm standing in yet another endless queue tomorrow... She has been to see Sis and James and, thank God, they are just about all right. Sis is incredibly clever at getting help from anywhere and anybody; she has always been that way. I can imagine how well she and Jetje got on together; they are two of a kind! Jetje tells me that James is doing fine. It is so good to know, especially when you hear what is happening all around that little boy. For example, trees have totally disappeared in the towns. Can you imagine those beautiful canals in our cities without their trees?

Wood for burning is so scarce now that people are chopping up the shelves off their walls, units from their kitchens and cupboards out of their living rooms for fuel, to be able to keep warm for just a few more days. Wooden coffins don't exist any longer: the dead are removed in cardboard boxes or even just in sheets.

And many people are dying. Outbreaks of illnesses like tuberculosis, dysentery and typhoid fever are spreading their tentacles everywhere and because there simply is not enough food to live on, thousands of people don't have a chance to recover and are starving to death.

On her way there Jetje saw rows and rows of people pushing or pulling any kind of vehicle, trying to get to the farms in the hope of collecting some food. There were wheelbarrows, prams, even dolls prams, and many decrepit old bicycles without tyres. She saw one man on a bike which did not have its proper front wheel any more so the tiny wheel of a child's bicycle had been fixed in its place. The man was cycling slowly, upright and full of dignity, but nobody laughed.

I am eternally grateful to Jetje and deeply happy to know that James is all right. I borrowed a mattress from Katja and insisted that I would sleep on that tonight down here and Jetje upstairs with Elsbeth. Elsbeth was delighted. The two of them planned an evening up there, telling stories to each other and Adriana was going to be the heroine in each one. I get the impression that Jetje adores that doll as much as the official owner!

I will lie down near the stove with its last bit of warmth still glowing and for once I think I'll sleep right through the night.

Isobel

April 1945
Heerenstraat

Hello Darling,

Great excitement this afternoon. Hendrik, our close friend and our doctor in the years when we lived in Vaassen, visited us for a special reason. He wanted me to be one of the first to hear his extraordinary story.

Yesterday, very early in the morning, he had been called by a farmer who lives close to the village. Late the previous night, an RAF plane had been hit by a German night fighter and it had come down in one of the fields near the farm house.

There were some cries for help from the plane, but as it was burning

123

fiercely the farmer was afraid it would explode, thinking that it might well be a bomber. Some time later he decided to go and have a look and there he found a man who had managed to escape the plane through an opening between the tail guns and then crawl away from the burning wreck. He was the only survivor.

The distinctive shape of a Lancaster, one of several bombers used by the RAF during WW2

The farmer, who didn't speak a word of English, took him to the farmhouse, where he made him as comfortable as possible. Because of the curfew, he was not able to call Hendrik until six in the morning.

The airman, a 30-year-old sergeant, was very relieved to be spoken to in English by Hendrik. He told him that he had managed to give himself a morphine injection from his first aid kit as soon as he had crawled a safe distance away from the plane, which had taken away all physical pain. Unfortunately, it had not been able to take away the agonising certainty that all his crew, with whom he had flown countless hours through countless nights, were dead.

Hendrik was well aware that this man was very weak, was badly burnt and needed much more medical care than he could give. All he could do was to make sure he was kept warm and quiet. The airman, however, wanted to keep talking. He brought out a rather crumpled packet of cigarettes from one of his pockets and offered one to Hendrik. A very precious gift!

Then he started to talk about his wife and children back in England; he described his house, his garden and his county, which was Kent.

Oh, how I would have liked to have been there, Jan Willem, and hear this Englishman describe that beautiful part of the country so close to my Surrey!

He gave Hendrik his address, which he has put carefully away. As soon as possible after the war he'll write to the poor man's wife and tell her what has happened to her husband.

After about two hours, during which the two of them thoroughly enjoyed several cigarettes, the Germans arrived to take him away as a prisoner of war. He begged Hendrik to stay with him as long as possible, but all Hendrik could do to help was to take off his coat and put it over the airman when the Germans placed him on a farm wagon to be taken to the village, and from there to the military hospital in the nearby town. From that moment it has been impossible to get any news about him.

Poor Hendrik, he has always hated not being able to do absolutely everything for a patient, even when he has done all he possibly could. This was particularly difficult because the airman was a patient being taken away from the farm where he had been comforted and from a doctor who had spoken and listened to him. Hendrik would have loved to have given him the treatment he so needed.

I'm really glad that he came to talk about what happened. It had obviously touched him very deeply, and no wonder; he had met one of the many men who are trying to liberate us, and seen the wreck of his plane with other members of the crew dead inside it. It was crushing to have a long conversation with someone who, in that small space of time, became a friend but was then taken away a prisoner... Even the farmer and his wife were pretty upset about it all and Hendrik stayed with them for quite a time, trying to calm them down, telling the farmer how well he had handled everything and how grateful everyone concerned was to him. We both thought this was such a special day that we had a cup of tea! I just used a few leaves – it was a much diluted small cup for each of us, but it

125

tasted wonderful.

It was interesting to hear about this airman, his wife and his two tiny boys. He had been a fruit grower before joining the RAF, working in his orchard in Kent, the county known as the Garden of England. He had described joining the RAF, his training and the first few times he had taken part in the night raids, feeling this extraordinary mixture of excitement and fear. And then he had said that he also, deep down, felt sadness that in order to liberate the occupied countries, another country had to be destroyed. He had never ever told anybody else about those feelings.

Hendrik had thought deeply before answering and then he said:

"I can so understand what has been going through your mind, but be assured that what you are destroying is an evil that is so close to hell that it is imperative it is stopped, not only for the rest of the world but also for the ordinary German people. And, after living with this evil for almost five years, to us, the Dutch, the RAF raids are the only visible manifestation of the war effort and the sound of the planes flying above us is a song of liberty."

He went home after our tea party in time to beat the curfew and now I am writing down what he said and realise again what a wonderful friend he is.

How I would love to talk about this with you tonight, but that isn't possible. All I can do is send you my love.

Isobel

April 1945
Heerenstraat

I sometimes wonder if I can keep going. It is hearing one distressing piece of news after the other that gets to you, today's being no exception.

126

It was Katja who brought it. Just after our daily lunch of thin, totally tasteless soup, Mary Jane had gone out with Hannie. Elsbeth was in the garden with the other children and I was mending, yet again, the navy blue top she has been wearing for years (the holes keep reappearing).

As soon as Katja came in I knew something serious had happened. Her face was drawn and white; it isn't true that white is not a colour, her face was cast with innumerable shades of sadness. She told me as gently as she could that Robert van Dijk had been arrested yesterday and shot early this morning. Robert! I could not imagine it. I could not understand it. I did not want to believe it. He had been a friend from the very beginning of our life in Apeldoorn. A judge, well known and deeply respected, his love of justice was so important to him that nobody was in the least surprised when he joined the Resistance early on. I don't know what work he was doing, of course I don't, but it was something to do with underground papers: those precious, thin, often just stencilled sheets, which tell us the truth, rather than the loud propaganda of the official press in German hands.

O, Jan Willem, for once I am glad I can't send you my letters, and I hope that it will take a long time before you hear this news. He and you got on so well together, both of you ever hungry for books, loving to talk about them together. There was poetry, there were novels, but both of you, above anything else, adored Shakespeare. You poured over play after play, taking them to bits in discussions and (to the embarrassment of your wives), quoting from them. Beautiful, clever – but very much showing off, Barbara and I thought, as did probably everybody else in the room! I can't begin to imagine what Barbara must be feeling at this moment.

I can't imagine either how Robert was caught; he was always so very careful, never taking any risk. There can only be one answer: he must have been betrayed. I would like to run and see Barbara straight away, but it would not be safe. She will be watched, just to find out who'll go to her and thereby show a possible trail to others who are on the wanted list.

What a very different Katja it had been who had run into our room in September 1944, full of excitement, crying:

"The Allies have landed in the south, the Germans are fleeing eastwards!"

It was the 5th of September, which came to be called 'Dolle Dinsdag' or 'Crazy Tuesday' forever after. We all believed that liberation was to reach us really soon, but it was not to be and we are still waiting and hoping.

Katja and I sat together for quite some time. We talked about Robert, this great man who had done so much during all those years of occupation. We are so near to the end of this horrible race, and now he will never touch the finishing line.

"God, I wish I could be as brave as he was" I said. And Katja answered softly:

"You are, you know. Remember Rosa?" Rosa. How will I ever forget? Tomorrow evening I will write it down.

Love you,
Isobel

April 1945
Heerenstraat

Darling, you know Rosa's story as well as I do, but I know I am right, it will be a very good thing to write it down. It might just calm the nightmares I still have about her.

It was in early July 1943 when one of our Quaker friends came to visit us. It was a pleasant surprise to see him and we were most happy to welcome him into our house. However, he seemed very serious and anxious. You asked him what was worrying him and he said he had come to see us because our help was needed.

One of the many things the Quakers have done from the very start of the war is to help the Jews, finding one safe address after another as sanctuary for them. I have no idea how many Jewish men, women and children have been spirited away by them, and we realised at once in what way our help was going to be needed: another Jewish person was seeking shelter from the ever present danger.

It was a 19 year old girl who needed protection; we were warned that she looked entirely Jewish and that she could be very strong willed and rebellious. Would we please think about it, but if possible not for too long because this was a pressing case. In the event it took twenty-six minutes, during which we had discussed it with each other and with the girls. Rosa was going to arrive in two days time.

We had two small bedrooms in our loft, one of which was Elsbeth's. The other was a typical junk room, full of boxes, suitcases, an old cupboard and all kinds of things we hardly ever used. We decided that Rosa should have Elsbeth's room, who would move in with Mary Jane, since she had quite a large room. This way we had Elsbeth, who was terribly excited about Rosa coming, close to her big sister who could keep her under control.

In the case of a rumour of a possible German visit to the house, Rosa could be hidden under the floor in the hall, where a space had been dug out. If it should happen when she was in her room up in the loft with no time to run down two flights of stairs (Dutch staircases are immensely long and steep!), the cupboard in the junk room would be her hiding place. This wasn't as safe as the hall, but with one of us locking the cupboard after her (you had put some air holes in the back), it was the best we could do.

We told the girls that the story would be that Rosa was a niece of yours, that she had had tuberculosis and had been sent by her doctor to our part of the country to get better. All this background had been worked out by the Quakers, who sent her to us. (She was even going to have the 'doctor's letter' on her), and both Mary Jane and Elsbeth were told to remember the story word for word.

When Rosa arrived we all fell under her spell. She had a warmth about her which lit up any room she walked into; meeting her, one would never have guessed what she had been through during those years of war. She had studied at the Academy of Music as a viola player; she was not just good, she was gifted. When she came to us she brought her instrument with her, and when she played the warmth and joy of her character flowed through each note.

She had lived with her parents in Amsterdam and the family had been warned that they must move into a hiding place at once. Her father stubbornly refused and in the autumn of 1941 Rosa, cycling into her road, was stopped by a neighbour.

"Don't go home," he said, "I am so very sorry, but the Germans have been and taken your parents. It's far too dangerous for you to go to the house."

"I must," she answered. "I must say farewell to each room and I must say goodbye to my parents, even though they are not there anymore. And also I must go and get my viola."

"Don't worry," she smiled, "I have a contact address. They will help me."

It was the Quakers who took her under their wing. Over the next few years she stayed in different homes. Sometimes she lived with people she felt really happy with, but there were also times when she felt out of place, lonely and unhappy. Whenever there was the slightest hint of the risk of discovery it became necessary to move her yet again. The only constant thing in her life was her viola, and even that had to be kept silent for months on end.

By 1943 it became more and more difficult to find safe homes in the west of the country. German soldiers hunting for Jews found their prey much more easily in the cities, where they could search house after house, street after street.

It was decided that it would be better to move Rosa to a quieter part of the countryside, which was when the Quakers approached us.

My Love, it's getting late. The days are really busy and I find myself looking forward to the evenings when I have time to write. I do believe that 'night time is thinking time', but this evening I am really tired and it is better to leave the rest of the story till tomorrow.

Until then, all my love,
Isobel

April 1945
Heerenstraat

My Darling,

It's been a good day. The sun has been shining, and I don't know how or why, but the soup kitchen produced quite a nice soup today with more potatoes than usual and even a few scraps of other vegetables in it. The three of us sat companionably in the garden this afternoon, reading and resting, so I feel really well tonight and eager to write more about Rosa.

Not a single German soldier searched our house while she was with us; she never needed to hide either in that cupboard or under the floor of the hall. It was an altogether different danger which changed everything. The Germans were becoming more and more uncertain of the superiority of their military power, and they feared a British invasion of the coast of Holland, so they decreed that the entire government infrastructure, still consisting of Dutch civil servants but entirely under German influence and control, must be moved away from The Hague in the west and established further east. We received an order to grant hospitality to one of these civil servants, quite a high-ranking one in fact. It was no use even thinking about refusal, one simply couldn't. Opposite us was a big building where he was to have his office, and all his underlings would be there as well.

We were told that Mr Hobbema was coming to our house on the Wednesday afternoon of the following week so that we could get to know each other. We could also then show him his room … Rosa's room. We had no idea what this Mr Hobbema would be like, but however decent he might turn out to be, we could never trust him not to betray Rosa. And then there was the chance that it could be far worse; this man might be a collaborator. Rosa would have to go.

We had a few days to play with. I went to see your mother, who lived a few streets away in a very select boarding house for elderly people. This apparently harmless place is also a hive of Resistance activity and the landlady, well into her sixties, walks around with a pistol in her bloomers, so I have been told. Knowing her, I quite believe it. I went along and talked with Mrs van Loenen about the problem, who said that as far as she was concerned it would be possible to house Rosa, but she had to put it to the residents of her home. Everyone would have to be totally happy about this.

It was discussed and, yes, Rosa could come! There were three conditions:

First: Everybody in the home would have to learn Rosa's story by heart, exactly the same way as our daughters had learned it.

Second: If there was any trouble, if anything came out, nobody, but *nobody* was to have realised that Rosa was Jewish.

Third: most important of all, Rosa was told never, *never* to go out.

So Rosa moved yet again, and just as with everywhere else, Rosa was liked and enjoyed by everyone in the home. All was well for a while, but then she fell in love with the young grandson of one of the residents; he came to the home quite often to visit his grandfather, and he and Rosa came to know each other. I have no idea if he was in love with her, but she certainly was with him, and she wanted to buy him a present. She went out and was arrested immediately.

Some time later, the young servant girl in the home looked out of the landing window and saw a German officer and a young Dutch collaborator on their way to the house. They had obviously 'spoken' to Rosa and knew where to come. The girl ran to your mother's room and told her what was happening. Your mother had rehearsed the story about Rosa again and again, but at that very moment she knew she would not be able to do it. She had deep faith and she started to pray, saying, "God, I won't be able to lie to these men, but please help me to say the right thing."

The two men came in and sat down. The German said nothing, he just listened; it was the Dutchman who asked the questions. Your mother answered, telling them the whole story: every name involved was mentioned, each address given – everything.

And then she went for them.

"What you are doing is absolutely wrong," she said. "All of us: me, my children, my son and his wife, are completely opposed to the way the Jews are treated. We, the Dutch, will fight for the very last Jew in this country, because what you are doing is totally against God's will."

There was a deep silence and then the young Dutch collaborator looked up at her and said, "Madam, my grandmother would have said exactly the same. You will not hear any more about this."

He whispered something to the German, they both got up and walked out and nothing was seen of them ever again. I still shiver when I think what could have happened to us all. More about poor Rosa tomorrow.

Always yours,
Isobel

April 1945
Heerenstraat

Darling,

You can imagine how scared we were for several days, expecting arrest at any moment, but nothing happened, and then a letter from Rosa arrived

133

at your mother's home; we simply could not believe it when she told us that Rosa had actually written to them. When she was arrested, she had been taken to the police station, where they interrogated her. While in her cell she wrote a letter to Mrs van Loenen, which began by saying how deeply sorry she was for what she had done, putting all the people involved in such terrible danger. The letter was smuggled out for her by a Dutch policeman who brought it to the home – another example of Resistance work.

Of course, none of us could answer it, none of us could tell Rosa about the miracle that had happened, that we were safe.

What strikes me each time I read the letter is the fact that she always refers to 'them', she could not bring herself to write the word 'Germans'. This is what she wrote:

The 1st Day

The fact that I am sitting here in Cell 3 is so utterly what I deserve, that I accept it without any demur.

I believed, but I was not certain of my faith in God during difficult moments. Now I have realised that every human being receives what he or she deserves. I have lost the wonderful life I had because of my own stupidity and carelessness. The lesson He gives me now is the right one and I fully accept that it is justified.

At the same time He gives me the sign that He exists. I trust in Him completely, and through that I am able to accept my fate, sure that He will give me the strength to endure even harder and more difficult hours, and that He will guide me in critical moments when I may not be certain what I should do.

I do not yet know why He does not give me the strength to take my own life.

Or is this, deep down, cowardice? Is it because of not

daring to admit my own stupidity that I want to die?

My deepest thanks to all those people who have been so indescribably good and loving to me; I was not worthy of it – may God protect them.

The 2nd Day

Why is it that, together with my feelings of acceptance towards God, I have such rebellious feelings towards certain people?

I feel that nobody can hurt me more than they have already done. I wish they would shoot me, but I know they won't: I have seen my identity card and it has a capital S stamped on it, S for 'Straffe', German for 'punishment'. That means I will be sent to Westerbork, that place in the north east of the country where all people like me are gathered, and then? I simply don't know.

I am not allowed to have a blanket any longer – well I am just grateful for the days when it was allowed and look, the sun has started to shine again! I can just glimpse it through my tiny window.

If God wants the best for me, He will help me, but I have not deserved it. It is not the beatings or even possible torture which will be the worst. The worst is the immense self reproach and regret I feel.

The small plant I have here in my cell, which I bought as a birthday present for somebody on the day I was arrested, is bending over more and more, owing to lack of sufficient light. I haven't reached that stage yet. O yes, I have bowed, but not for them, only for God.

And I shall never break.

May God forgive me for this, but His commandment

135

to "love our enemies", is something I can now no longer obey. When I die, I shall not die for them, but simply because I don't deserve to live any longer. May those who have been brought into danger through my stupidity, forgive me.

The 3rd Day

I get sufficient and good food each day, even without my coupons. The Dutch policemen are kind to me – at least as far as they are permitted to be.

My old habit of viewing everything too rosily is beginning to assert itself again. I find myself even looking at things from the funny side ….though there is not much that is funny here.

After my meal I lie flat on my back on my plank-bed, just dreaming about the food I've had and at the same time singing all Beethoven's symphonies to myself. One by one. How I would love to have my viola, but singing will have to do and is it not a miracle that I can do that under the circumstances?

Writing with the paper on my lap is not very easy; it is difficult to do it neatly, but most probably nobody will ever read this. It just passes the time.

Fortunately one of the policemen has given me a rather nice book to read. I have a touch of rheumatism in my shoulder, most likely because of the rather damp atmosphere in here, but never mind.

It sounds strange perhaps, but actually I am deeply grateful that my parents have gone before me. My darling mother could never have borne the knowledge that her one and only child is in this cell. If she is still alive today, then she will be thinking of me with joy, remembering the many and wonderful hours we had together and convinced that I am somewhere in Holland, healthy and happy.

The 4th Day

When will I leave here? I don't know. I could quote Multatuli (my school teacher would be pleased to know I remembered the words written by his favourite author!): "I do not know where I will die and still less, how."

The more I think about it, the more I realise that people, especially recently, have been extremely kind to me. Some of them did not even know precisely who I was.

How did I deserve this? I feel so ashamed towards them. Perhaps it is just as well I won't see them ever again, I would not know how to face them. I hope they can forgive me. I am certain that God has already done so, because I am as penitent as a lamb. Perhaps that is why, even under the circumstances I have not lost my positive thinking.

When I start thinking of all the friends I have lost, all the children I knew who have disappeared during these last few years – all the people I loved so much, then, no, nothing happens, there is emptiness. I immediately put those thoughts out of my mind and say to myself: "I won't think of that any more today, perhaps tomorrow…"

Or will there not be another day for me tomorrow?

Well, then I will give up the fight. However courageously I started to play the match, I will have to admit that I have lost. I won't have any regrets: a match can be played in a beautiful and fair way without necessarily winning it. And my latest years, despite all the hurt, have been beautiful, something I can only be grateful for.

I think if I reread all of these pages I've written, I would laugh at the sentimental idea:

"Last thoughts of a young girl who died
in the bloom of her years."

I am not like that at all, I would never think like that. But when you are trying to put your thoughts down on paper, sitting in a cell, you can't very well write about sweet nothings or discuss the weather – all I know about that, is that it is cold.

The 5th Day

Just now something nice happened. A young man, who escaped from a work camp and has been put in Cell 1, managed to give me some biscuits. They don't taste very nice, but all the same I am very grateful for them. It's the wonderful way such a gift is given. It is obvious: men don't like seeing a woman behind bars. It's a little bit like a film drama, and indeed the last few years have been quite dramatic.

I will very likely be going to Westerbork tomorrow.

It was never my idea to have these pages "published" (as the smart people call it), and yet I would dearly like it if some of my acquaintances and friends, who are without any doubt very disappointed in me, will not think too badly of me. I shiver at the thought of innocent people being in danger because of what I have done.

So perhaps it is right that I will suffer the same fate as so many others. Forgive me, dear, dear people.

I will stop writing now. For whom this letter is intended, I don't know. I do so hope that Mrs van Loenen will be able to read it with understanding, and also and above all the old lady and her family, for whom I pray each day. I do hope you don't think this just sentimental – it is genuine.

Once again my thanks for the love and kindness I have been given.

Your deeply grateful, sad and yet thankful
R.

April 1945
Heerenstraat

My darling Jan Willem

Everybody is saying it, that it will soon be over. No longer will I need to sit down in the evenings and write. All I will do now is put down the thoughts I had during last night:

"The darkness deepens as I lie in bed thinking over what has happened during the day and what may or may not happen tomorrow.

And then I hear it – far away a soft humming sound, coming nearer and nearer. It grows louder – becomes a droning noise and suddenly it is a great roaring sound above our heads – and there they are once more – the Allied aircraft, flying across the flat fields of Holland on their way to Germany, those young men, risking their lives for the liberation of the occupied countries – for *us* and for the maintenance of democracy in a free world.

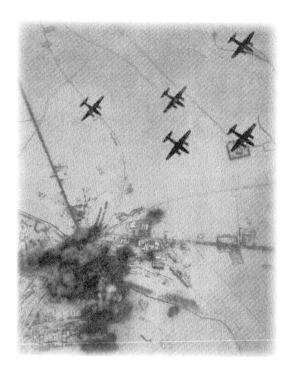

And I am filled with feelings of enormous gratitude towards those brave men; and also a feeling of wonder and astonishment that they are really there, that they exist, that there really is a free England across the North Sea, not so far away in distance but oh so far away because of the impossibility of any contact whatsoever with my native land. And so the roaring sound gradually dies down to a hum and then to a faint whisper... But we in occupied Holland are filled once again with hope: we know that very soon victory will be achieved and we shall at last be liberated and free to live as decent human beings once more."

God bless you and send you home soon
Isobel

Liberation!

EPILOGUE

On 17 April 1945 our town was liberated by the Canadians under the command of General Major H.W. Foster CBE DSO. That was the day that Isobel stopped writing her letters; there was no more need.

Her family was able to return to their old house in the Rozenlaan and directly opposite, the Canadians erected their barracks and I (Elsbeth in the book) was allowed to have breakfast with the Canadian soldiers every morning. I must have behaved well, because not only was I 'adopted' into their army, I was promoted to 'Captain of Signals'. Having married an Englishman and lived in England for nearly fifty years, I still have the jacket on which my mother sewed the insignia.

After the war, James came home. Some very difficult years followed, with his epilepsy becoming worse. Following years of searching, the right place was found: at the age of twenty-two he joined a Rudolf Steiner home where he blossomed into a talented man with a gift for music and poetry. He learned to transpose and even to compose music, and he wrote poems, some of which were amusing, some deeply moving. No wonder one of the leaders in the home instigated his receiving the Dutch equivalent of the MBE. He died in 2007. On his gravestone it says, "Musician, Poet – and so much more."

Mary Jane became a Social Worker, married and had two little boys. I wish I could say much more about her but tragically, at the age of thirty, she died of breast cancer, when her younger child was only one year old.

Years after the war, having retired as a Mechanical Engineer, Jan Willem wrote an article for a magazine, following which he received a letter from Amsterdam. It said, "I am so thankful to have discovered, through reading your article, that you are still alive: I was one of the children you rescued. Just outside Jerusalem is the *Anne Frank Park* in which trees are planted to commemorate those who helped Jewish children during the war years. One of those trees is there because of what you did."

Isobel lived until the age of ninety-nine, still looking beautiful. She and Jan Willem lived on in Holland where, in 2001, they celebrated their 73rd wedding anniversary with their children, grandchildren and ten great-grandchildren.

There is a memorial stone in the dunes in Holland on which a text by Van Randwijk is chiselled. Some of the words translate as follows:

"During the occupation of The Netherlands, from the midst of the nation, men and women stood up. Peace loving people became arsonists, saboteurs and spies. They kept the free word alive through illegal papers and helped the persecuted. Many died in prison or in front of the firing squad.

Remember that what was threatened yesterday, might to-day or tomorrow be in danger again. Guard it and be watchful."